T0380197

# POEMS FROM THE CWTCH

## SUE A'HERN

authorHOUSE

*AuthorHouse™ UK*
*1663 Liberty Drive*
*Bloomington, IN 47403  USA*
*www.authorhouse.co.uk*
*Phone: 0800.197.4150*

*Published by AuthorHouse  10/02/2017*

*ISBN: 978-1-5462-8287-7 (sc)*
*ISBN: 978-1-5462-8311-9 (e)*

*Print information available on the last page.*

Dear Reader,

I've had a brain aneurism and other disabling medical conditions, and now are coming the complications of getting older. I have temporal Dementia, long and short term memory loss; simple tasks are getting more difficult to execute. My ability to write poetry is starting to wane, I fear that pretty soon it will gone, but hopefully I won't be able to remember I've lost the skill. I don't have a specific style or genre of writing, I tend to go for whatever style the topic requires. All my poems are based on my daily and long term life experiences, this book contains mostly the last year of my life; a memoir in poetic form. So as I begin to fall gradually from power this book is dedicated to all those who have unwittingly become a part of 'Poems From The Cwtch', in particular K who is the last person with whom I've had a romantic and tumultuous relationship. So that's me, an old bird with a brain that exploded, who is confused about a million things, and getting more muddled and bewildered with each passing day. So as one of my lost friends would say – Get stuck in.

Good health and a big thank you for reading my poetry,

Yours sincerely,

Sue A'Hern

# INTRODUCTION

Could say I'm a poet
Who doesn't know it
I'm a bit of a twat
But everyone knows that.

As you put your fingers in the page
Don't let the odd fuck make you rage
Some of it's got a hidden meaning
Read between the lines for further gleaning.

It's not stuff that'll make you horny
In fact some of it should touch you warmly

It's a bit of this and that a bit no bother
Genital driven in tiny teeny part and a bit of the other.

Mostly it's just words on a page
Shouldn't be too much to cause a rage
If you're offended by the verb fuck
Read the rest and avoid the muck.

# COCOA AND VELVET AVATAR

(For Abbey M-W)

Here she comes, all sinew, muscle and tan,
Woven inside a tightly coiled spring;
Her velvet skin inducing reactions of
Avarice and warmth, combined with lust and envy.
She's gentle of mouth and foot,
Humble in her own assertive way;
With an exuberance she keeps hidden inside.

For those of us reaching our sell by date,
And approaching or past mid-life crisis;
She is a reminder of how sweet life can taste,
How not one more second,
Should be left to dwindle.
Whilst there are still a million little things,
That when ignited can burn within.

There's a lucky person out there,
Somewhere way behind the scenes;
With the privilege of igniting
Her litmus paper,
Observing how her colours change.
Testing the limits and the range
Of a Cocoa and Velvet Avatar.

# DEMOTED ANGEL NYMPH

Tutelary ethereal spectre of folklore and romance,
Ultimately seeking solace deep in bluebell woods,
Legend of flights of fantasy and romance.
One of yet another conquered diminished race.
Transparent on wing leaving a trail of sparkling dust.
Human in appearance completely independent of race.
Many protect from your malice with cold iron,
Avoid offence by shunning where you inhabit.
Demoted angel spirit of the air
Caught between heaven and hell.
Hidden spectre of glade and woodland
Where baby's first laughter falls.
With dry bread in my pocket you are welcome,
Accept my offering of cream and butter.
Tell freely your name and grant me your powers,
There will be no forced bidding.

# DISEASE OF REMISSION AND RELAPSE

Beyond anything the imagination can create
Each anniversary as fresh as the last,
His scent in the air still present and real.
Images of anniversary day held close in their frame
Inanimate objects kept for their essence.
Distantly gone and long since passed,
Reminiscent days bring loves longing
Out of the clutter free corner
Where the reunion is still expected.
Time of remission with this disease
Never shortened nor gentler in relapse,
Symptoms worsen as the date arrives
Lingering eternally from remission to relapse.

# THE CRYING DREAM

In the crying dream, you were there,
I screamed at you but no sound came out.
You didn't see me, I shouted in your face,
I am here!
Look at me please,
You ignored me, didn't react once.
You walked right through me,
I curled up in ball, sobbed uncontrollably.
When I looked up, you were laying on a sofa,
Drinking a cup of tea.
I begged and begged and pleaded,
Please hear me, see me please.
You looked right through me,
With no expression,
Not a flicker of recognition.
I shook and sobbed,
I put my arms around you, tried to bring you close.
You were like stone, you couldn't feel me.
You got up, walked right through me,
Left and slammed the door.
I tried to run after you,
But my legs just wouldn't move.
I tried to force a jump; eventually my legs left the floor.
But I hadn't moved an inch forward.
I sat on the floor and cried and cried some more.

# MIDSUMMER DREAM

Titania beckons the dreamer forward
With long fine fingers she takes hold.
As we move through the forest in silence
Surreal and bizarre animals strike curios poses
Their doe eyes sometimes in hesitance make brief contact.
The Fairy Queen's grip is firm but tender,
As bluebells are trod underfoot
Confused emotions rise and fall.
Concern and hesitance fall into safe and calm,
Melancholic and magical,
Pastel colors all around.
Happy at being led by such a fine hand
The slow walking continues calmly all night.

# SNAKES AND DOGS DREAM

(1)

The canvas bag across my shoulder hangs heavy at my hip
Its contents wriggle and move
A number of large dogs pull ahead
The leather strap around my wrist hurts and chaffs
As they pull I strain to keep their pace
Being pulled by them along a slippery jetty
I struggle to stay on my feet
The focus is to reach an old wooden hut on the end
As the dogs pull nearer the dwelling
They begin to slaver and breathe heavy
I put my hand in the bag
Pull out handfuls of wriggling snakes
And hurl them at the hut with all my might
The dogs are now off the lead
Much to my frustration they have lost interest
They run around barking and playing
Meanwhile the snakes slither off the jetty into the sea.

# SUNK SHIP DREAM

(2)

Over half the ship is sunk
Only it's overly large mast is completely above water
Green slime and barnacles cover it
Almost at the top of the mast clinging is a must
Feet and fingers dig into the rotting wood
They are sore from splintered grip
The sea beneath hurls itself about
As the ship rocks the grip momentarily loosens
Before a tight hold is once again gained
Sometimes she is relaxed and observant
When she is not she feels triumphant
There is no panic or fear clinging is just a task
Sometimes the woman on the mast is me
And sometimes I am the observer
We are always content.

**(3)**

Now and then the Sunk Ship Dream
Is an integral part of the Snakes and Dogs Dream
Depending on if I am she or she is me
Or if I am an observer to both
The format slightly changes but the theme remains.

# FEATHER SPITTING OLD

Days crow feather spitting old
When the subconscious self is bold,
Beauty sleep scares as it falls
And ugliness scarily unfolds.

The hidden depths of paranoia
Freed to grow even wilder,
To shout and to squeal
It's not paranoia it is real.

Daylight brings a lift into a chair
At inner eyelids left to stare,
Soaked sponges wet dry lips
Administered are chemical tricks.

Another day crow feather spitting old
With no response to are you cold,
Suck on that wet sponge my dear
Here's more chemicals for that fear.

# FEEL, BE, MOVE, DANCE...

Sing out sympathetically,
Feel the melody played,
Let the sound entrance,
Take rhythm into bone,
Be moved by the sound.

Feel allured
Feel enticed
Feel infused
Feel engaged
Feel privileged

Dance without shame,
Flourish in movement,
Enjoy the swaying,
React with your body,
Move it spin it around.

Be outpouring
Be moving
Be engaging
Be blooming
Be enchanting

Sway and slide about,
Move hips from side to side,
Come in real close,
Shimmy from head to toe,
Let it flow and take you.

Move with impulsion
Move with explosion
Move with perception
Move with seduction
Move with sensation

Take it to another level,
Move a cog up or down,
Let your body do the talking,
Express from inside out,
Be at one with the rhythm.

Dance unconditionally
Dance seductively
Dance unreservedly
Dance happily
Dance contently…

# FIFTEEN MINUTES OF PAGE 3 POETRY FAME

The photograph and the article took up a whole half a page
The Evening Post provided her with fifteen minutes of fame.
On the day of the publication a quiet cup of herbal tea and toasted tea cake in a café
Turned to sideward glances, pointing fingers and recognition,
A Page three girl joke followed by a nod and a wink.

Proof in words do matter,
Releasing her work of poetry
She is able to express herself
And it's available to buy now.

After a serious illness her career came to an abrupt halt,
The painstaking rehabilitation processes all aided recovery and progression.
The Poet says;
'When I awoke from the coma I didn't know who I was, didn't even recognize my children.
I needed to be back in familiar surroundings, where I can remember every street; the poems are based
on my life, about everything really.'

The article ends with a few words from the poet, says so much about her struggle for identity.
'I am not just Sue who used to work at a university and is ill anymore.'
The Poet if indeed that's what she now is
Took a quick bow in her fifteen minutes of fame
Scurried back to her isolation and work station
Before beginning once more over again.

# WORSE IS YET TO COME

Flood of Predictable Unpredictability
Indian summers and arctic winters
Shrinking sea ice the cause of evacuation.

Thermal imaging gives clear indication
Fire service worked throughout the night.

Debris and danger revealed and removed.

Trapped in his car
The man died.

River banks gave way
Too mud slide and water.

Winds at 96 miles an hour
Time and speed of the essence.

Fire crews searched rubble
Some thought trapped.

30 day's worth
Fell in 36 hours.

Back edge of cloud
Allowed colder air to creep in.

Transportation by boat arranged as
Homes and gardens became lakes.

Shrubs under water and
. Daffodil bulbs afloat.

Swans and ducks take advantage
Not be chased away.

TV and stereo
Never to work again.

Insurance assessors
Spoke of hundreds of thousands.

Storms battered overnight
Motorists beware.

Inevitability of disruption.

There was standing still
There was chaos.

Historic properties
Not saved.

Gardens slid
Down muddy slopes.

Improper drainage
Lead the way to
Demolition balls a coming.

Worse is yet to come
Advice is be cautious.

# FLOWER GARDEN Q&A

Mary Mary quite so contrary how's the garden these days?
"A full servicing is only a phone call away."

Gloriala Glory petals of blonde have you had luck lately?
"Not for a while but on a promise just the now."

Flory Flower your stem is broken but does the rest still work?
"No suitable experimental gardener found but still hopeful."

Rose Red you had a good weeding of late?
"Last creepers still climbing around my open gate."

Daisy Day are you still closed for business at night?
"Yes but I'm open all day it's so much better in the sun."

Rose Red thorny and velvet had any romance of late?
"Last creepers still on the go wound around my gate."

Jazzy Jasmine you sweet smelling thing is luck still with you?
"As ever still reaching for the sky intoxicating perfume works for me."

Red Hot Poker you old devil how'd you sneak in?
"Standing erect that's the key to attraction, my seeds everywhere,
I'm just eyeing up your friends."

# FOR HIM

Let me know
If not to bother,
Don't lurk around
And quietly hover.

Cut me free
With a feather,
To go and bathe
In more glorious weather.

Don't touch my hand
When you invite me in,
If all that's wanted
Is original sin.

No brushing of hand
Against my skin,
Trying to draw out
What's not within.
Speak out loud
Don't try to be clever,
I'm just a friend
Will give out never.

For my tested patience
Is worn thin,
With playing games
Where none can win.

I'm letting you know
I need a friend not lover,
Don't waste your time
Go find some other.

# POETRY GROUP - HEROES AND HEROINES

Are we not all heroic in our own way?
For me getting out of bed and facing the day feels like an act of heroism.

I don't know about you
You might fervently disagree
But there have been numerous times when I have donned a mask
Girded my loins
Felt the fear and strolled right in anyway
In what has felt like a heroic act.

I imagine we could debate the definition of hero or heroine
Until one of us spells it without the e on the end
And a whole new topic for debate is started
Or until one of us reaches a heroic hiatus and goes blue in the face.

Years ago I would tell my children
When I grow up I'm going to be Indiana Jones
Hoping that one day they might see
The heroic acts of fighting tyranny and oppression
Though way back then when I first said
I'm gonna be Indiana Jones when I grow up
They only saw Harrison Ford in the films
But I suppose Mr Ford is a hero of sorts.

Recently I've become acquainted with a woman called Flame
He as She has bared his soul in biographical form
Dannie has become a heroine to me in both masculine and feminine form
It really takes some heroic balls
Excuse the pun
To say to the world this is who I am
These are my words
My life laid out in black and white.

Is there not a Boudicca or a Lion heart lurking in our personalities?
All it takes is for the right buttons to be pressed
Or an accidental comment or action
To release the principal character, champion, exemplar.

High sentiments don't always make a hero of us
But they do often offer heroism in the labor and intention
Of the blood and sweat in tears of sadness and sheer complete joy.

Because I stand before you today, or sit as the case may be
And tell you I understand the Heroic couplet
Containing two lines of poetry one after another
That they rhyme and usually contain ten syllables and five stresses
That I've failed to construct a satisfactory heroic couplet myself
Might that make me a hero because I tried?

In the higgledy-piggledy world of admiration and hero worship
Do you feel compelled to give me a nudge off my dodgy pedestal?
I might in retaliation feel the urge hold up my poetry book
And say
Look at the evidence suck on that if you can.

But if there is something I have learned
It's that critics and experts usually start a critique with
I think…
If as a critic you believe what you say
Try using a more concrete form such as
I know…
I believe…
I understand…

So now are you looking at me and thinking
Is she ever going to shut up?
Or maybe more hopefully thinking
Yeah she's on the right track.

Whatever!

If you like it or not
You are my heroes and heroines
Coz you've had the guts to turn up and share your words
Now turn and smile at the hero next to you
And be smiled at coz you're a hero to.

As for me I got out of bed
Faced the day
Turned up
Told you I failed at Heroic Couplets
And read you this
Surely that's enough heroics for one day.

# HIDE IT INSIDE

However and when attraction drives,
I and we our needs must hide
Deep behind a fragile disguise;
Encased in the nuance of a moment.

It can wear so easily thin,
This delicate and brittle outer skin.

In moments of test and examination,
Nothing can taint the liberation of
Subtly feeling the lust sensation;
Incorporating attraction and distraction
Desire rules when attraction drives.
Expect the unexpected hidden inside.

# HUNCHBACK WITH TWO BACKS

That's the spot under that tree
High up on the bank
Egg met seed there.

He's quite the young man
Unbelievable how time flies
No more jumping locked gates
Canoodling under trees in the dark
However, it is on the to be repeated bucket list.
Bet they have CCTV now
And not chained cups, but unchained dogs
Can see the evening post headlines now
Knackered old dear arrested in park.

In my youth, such acts were fun, daring
Not considered perverse, obscene.

There would be many a two backed hunchback
Happy, carefree and in love under the stars.
Eating chips from the uplands on the way home.

Perhaps somewhere out there tonight
Another egg and seed meet in the park
Romance and promise filling the air
Kissing and canoodling, ah yes I remember it well.

# IN THE GARDEN OF MISADVENTURE

Why me?
Arguably why not?
Juxtaposed bad fortune,
And excremental luck,
In sublime trifling unreality
Of a meek mouthed casualty,
Glancing at,
The sleepy eyes of psychotherapy;
Telling a shaggy dog story.
Syntactically disapproving
With querulous synaesthesia.
Forbidding well justified
Expressions,
In funny peculiar bunk-hum,
Of willy-nilly
Wild card proportions of
Not Ha Ha
Peculiar.
The glottal stop of recognition
Way over wonder,
Reasoning for purpose
Agrees with suggestion;
Be aware,
Be very aware.
The mind occupying space
With persuasion,
In the garden of misadventure;
Misaligned by remote sensing,
Demanding to know,
Why me?
Arguably why not?
Is another question
Answered with a question.
So rude,
With no apology.

In the garden of misadventure,
Annular mouth muscle discharges,
Regurgitates,
Into a sick bucket;
Why me?
Arguably why not?

# INTOXICATING MOONSHINE

Lubrication for my aching soul,
that is what I find in you.
I have found what I've been looking for,
a crucial conceptual bit of meaning.
With a touch of deep passion,
and a sense of inner magic.

Lubricant for life
Providence with passion inside
Magical enjoyable

Cherry blossom for the mind,
that is what you are.
With a sweet heady scent,
your aroma intoxicates me.
The pollen that you omit,
is deeply absorbed into me.

Blossoming cherry scent
Containing pollen on wind
Breathing happiness

Fireworks for my heart,
that is what you bring.
A touch sparkling on my flesh,
like rockets in clear November skies.
Exploding against a full moon,
with warm exciting fulfilment.

Intoxicating light
Luscious moonshine exploding
Bringing light to darkness

Stars reflected in my eyes,
that is what you see.
The windows to my soul,
thrown open in glory.
Bright with shinning joy,
a reflection of you.

Looking deeply at id
Seeing your belonging there
Mirrored in reflection.

# LEAKING TIME AND MEMORY

So what does it matter,
Underneath it all
Sometimes the smart arse
Actually forgets her place,
Not that that really matters.

After all who's listening anyway?
However much nonsense comes out,
Everyone only hears what they want
Remembers their own version of events,
No leaking brain excuse for them.

What's the point in the incessant pressure?
I remember this you remember that,
To and fro the memory game goes
Half ways a good spot to meet and agree.

At the end of the day who gives a damn!

Let's play a game called
Explain experience and understand,
Assume my shoes and walk for a while,
Known for five minutes how different
Your memories and abilities are from mine.

Bloody hard isn't,
Refraining from having good memory,
And having thoughts extremely fatigue you
Isn't easy to get your head around,
Neither is explaining it to people.

Juxtapositions not positioned close together
Understanding harder and explaining more so,
So why not just take it as it is
That's a that is that kind of thing.

Time is irrelevant,
Is it 2.30am 6.45pm or 12 on the dot
Makes no difference to memories,
Either way it's gone coming and going.

What's the point in knowing your age?
Assumption is you're an idiot if you don't,
So better to pretend and hope for best
Tomorrows a different time anyway.
Inconsequential nonsense comes to the foreground,
No-one notices and someone often does,
Good luck making sense of it all.


Many ancestors have had the same,
Excavation and clamped condition
Multiple and single eruptions,
Of leaky worn out parts of brain.
Remembering them not possible,
Yet so many expect it to happen.

Just accept the memory and things as they are
Understanding it's for those possessing effort,
Nice people who are willing to take the chance.
Knowing it is harder than knowing about it,
If we all should live long enough
Explaining might happen in time.

# LIFE DRAWING CLASS

**The facilitator**
Followed guidelines:
Recap and reinforcement of learning,
Seven and a half heads as average
Eight in the graceful noble ideal
Eight and a half for the hero with a bigger chest and longer legs.

Introduction to session aims to introduce:
Weight of tone and line illustrating where flesh connects with flesh and hard surface.
The dramatic use of chiaroscuro
Strong contrast in use of light and dark tones,
Illustrated in Leonardo's sketches
Examples of Caravagio's use of light from dark.

Encouraged into the Vitruvius pose
Learners feel for themselves
The pressure on their feet
The weight from arm pit to wrist
The tension in neck, buttocks and hips.

**The Model**
Every inch a glory of Florence disrobes and stands on plinth
The Greek Adonis a striking resemblance to David,
Quiet and still as his marble doppelganger settled in the familiar pose.
Mathew the archetype of beauty nods his locks of curls
Indicating the onslaught of fingers sliding up and down tools,
Burnt willow scratching cartoon, squirrel hair and pigment on paper.

At the end of the session he observes the group critique,
Listens to the facilitator give instruction for research and tools needed for next session.
Amongst the bustle of portfolios and tool boxes
In anonymous faded blue jeans and black T-shirt
He collects his payment and leaves.

**The Learners**
Collate and store away handouts, notes and statements from critique,
Carefully wash equipment and pack away tools,
Place modellos, sketches, studies and finished pieces into leather portfolios,
Put semi dry canvases onto drying racks.

Take their additional learning recommendation to the café
Make rough sketches of kinaesthesia to enhance sense of the perception of movement.
Before attending Art History where the Topic is Michelangelo and Renaissance Art.

# LOCK AND OVERLOAD

Valedictory speeches of sensationalism
flow with permanent effervescence;
in a pre-prepared swansong statement
with underscored bullet points.
Impetuous sensational fervour
blankets the well-trodden common ground;
in a manner that habitual rules dictate
blindfolds are on and gloves are off.
Quintessential polite interactions
of a cordial ceasefire;
transform to lock and overload
take aim fire perturbation.
Ammunition of gymnastic exactitude
reloads and repeat fires;
until the art of polite interaction
turns to white noise.
Being neither ornament nor utensil
with variable unimportance and profit;
it can never be over and done
except just for now.

# LUMP FREE 38C'S

38c's are now more back than front
Like height they've reduced with age,
The Scammel wheel nut remark
Still applies on a cold winter's day.
Clamped between radiologists plates
No longer a melon, but a squashed grape,
Its partner gazes at the floor,
Head hung in shame.
Two sad pebbles red and flattened
Return to the safety of the over the shoulder boulder holder.
Back in the waiting room, urge resisted,
To stroke, and mold and say there there.
Posters on the walls illustrate technique;
Raise arm
Divide into sections
Feel with palm.
Young crisp white uniform
All pert and firm
Sends all clear 38c's away to fight another day.

# LOST IN THE FILM STRIP OF LIFE

Being lost in the film strip of life is a situation with a strict limit,
No identifying any potential for escape being fastened deep within it.
Wandering in the mists and dense forestation of a self-created wilderness,
Numbs the senses and creates a place within which there is no fun or happiness.
How does one climb out of a hole that is in danger of collapsing in,
Time to be brave and place the bet, sit back and wait for the win.
Gambling, they say is a game played only by fools,
So what else is there to do when you have lost your tools?
Hope is the only friend, and try and try as they may,
I cling to it tightly and they cannot take it away.
Forty eight hours or so to go and the chance is in sight,
But can I brave the strength of their miserable might.
Can they hold me back, can they keep control.
Will they want to or be able to block my shot at goal.
Head down and in I must charge, I must still protect my head.
I must be prepared to lie in it once I make the bed.
The chance to have a space to think is just a few days away,
Hopes must stay high; I must fight the dark and keep defeat at bay.
Hope is a term that bothers me; it plagues my troubled mind,
It comes and goes it peaks and troughs, as my plans begin to unwind.
Go there anyway and take the chances,
Don't look back, ignore their glances.

# MARY HAD A HABIT

(To the tune of Mary Had a Little Lamb)

Mary had a habit its fleece was white as snow
And every time that Mary sneezed the hole was sure to grow.
She took it to the office one day, this was against the rules
Her boss got really angry for being made a fool.
And so the manager turned her out, and whispered in her ear
That'll teach you junky to bring that snow in here.
Why does Mary love that stuff, her colleagues all did cry
Her drugs councilor asked the same question, and Mary couldn't reply.

# LITTLE MISS WANT IT

(To the tune of Little Miss Muffet)

Little miss want it
Bought for pure comfort
Eating her way through the day
The doctor whose was wiser
He tried to advise her
Comfort eating wasn't the way.

Little miss want it
Filled up her closet
Buying clothes every payday
The banker who spied her
A more credit advisor
Brought bankruptcy into her day.

Little miss want it
Lost her score for credit
Now charity shopping's her way
The skinny woman inside her
Stopped her getting wider
Reduced calorie for dinner again today.

Little miss want it
No longer compliant
The modern woman in every way
New education revived her
Now older and wiser
Than she was yesterday.

# HARK HARK

(To the tune of Hark Hark the Dogs Do Bark)

Hark Hark the wild dogs sing
Following the scent to town
Some in suits and some in jeans
And one in a pure silk gown.

34

# CRY BABY CAN'T COME IN

(To the tune of Cry Baby Bunting)

Cry baby hunting
Can't find what's a wanting
You keep knocking but you can't come in
No matter how grazed knuckles skin.

# MISS DEMEANOR

Mr Meena squeaky and cleaner
A man in a hat for special occasions
No arms to speak of or flay with
Long fat thumbs twenty in all
Belly resembles an enormous whoopee ready to blow
Legs as long as striped woollen stockings
Feet round and spoked a rolling rhyme
A not so gentleman most queerious
Accompanied oft by Miss Terious
Marvelling at his own mendaciousness
Most wonderful in his profound excellence
Eating bowls of sweet and sour innocence
Licking clean with no consequence
Neither pips nor stain on his pearly whites
Mr Meena forever to be superior
Shiny white detergent clean.

# MOBILE FROCKS

When she shouted Huw – Weeee…
I held her hair from her face,
When my head spun
She put my foot on the floor.
Once we got stranded in a snow drift,
Locked arms huddled close to keep warm.
When none of us was in real need
We agreed to faddy food diets,
Drank vegetable soup for a week,
(Compensating for too much alcohol).

After a Chumbawamba gig
We tub thumped all the way home,
While Aunty I's stolen decorated xmas tree
Rattled in the back of the van.

You taught me how to make a lentil pie,
I taught you to sew and mend.
We life modelled together,
Joked four tits for the price of two.
With our Mobile frocks dream catcher logo
We sold clothes bought cheap from Bruce.

Men and their offspring
Put pay to Mobile Frocks,
I wonder do you still think of me
My long lost friend
As I often do of you.

# MR SURGEON

Put me down for a head transplant please,
And whilst I'm under, give me new knees;
That I might squat, if I so please.

Because these days I tend to whir and wheeze,
A couple of new lungs, to breathe with ease;
And run a marathon, if I so please.

And while you're at it fix my mammories,
Nothing too big, nothing with sleaze;
Just enough, for the eye to please.

Mr Surgeon if you could please,
Get rid of all these personalities;
I'd like to have, just one of these.

# MS. HANDY-PERSON

Smiling a partial wanderlust grin,
she warns that she can bite,
before she invites you in;
to see what's behind
those cool pool blue eyes,
come swim they say see what you'll find.

Beneath the persona of confrontation,
and her batting for the other side,
lifelong committed affiliation;
with arms folded tight across
her years of liberation,
with Ms. Handy-Person there's no mistaking.

In every step she owns her destiny,
just watch how she walks,
it's plain to see;
that she's not the type to wear a dress,
though I have imagined it,
to that I confess.

I try to give nothing away,
as she crosses my path
on the occasional day;
but I think maybe it's too late,
I've already gone and opened
that closed floodgate.

To a world thought left behind,
thinking about re-entering
myself I find;
likely not with Ms. Handy-Person herself,
but just taking me down,
one last time off this dust filled shelf.

To be so old and still unsure,
of what I am
and to what exactly I allure;
all these thoughts they alarm,
as my quiet little life
they enter and disarm.

Ms. Handy-Person do you know,
that dormant seeds you've watered,
but will they grow?
in your van do you have a crystal ball?
that can tell me, will I hide away?
will I walk tall, or will I fall?

# MULTI GRAVID

Tiny fragile premature baby
No heavier than two bags of sugar
Determined to survive.

Sweet little lively baby
Bang on time easily birthed
Hungry from the start.

Big heavy determined baby
Overdue and face up
Grown up from day one.

Bright eyed sleepy baby
Mucus clogged in lungs
A fighter from the beginning.

Crying loudly baby
Angry with the world
Seeking more from first scream.

Long and heavy intelligent baby
Older from day one
Bright from first breath.

There is nothing that I won't have heard before;
Didn't you have a television?
Never heard of contraception?
Have you worked out what causes it yet?
And the endless jokes about liking sex.

And the inevitable questions come;
Some simply ask – why?
The foolish even ask – how?

Statically the odds are stacked
Against those from large families.
If you believe statistics,
At least one should be gay,
One might even be a murderer,
One might be in the care profession,
One will have a large family themselves,
And so on and so on…

# MUSCLE TUBE AND BEYOND

(Vaginal History List)
Seal intact
One finger
Two digits
Foreign object enquiry
Real thing
Entry failure
Second attempt
Docking successful
Apgar score
Shirodkar Sutures
More Apgar scores
Smear tests
Transcervical Resection
Hysterectomy
Moss growth
Skin thinning
Shape change
Waiting list
Prolapse
Monologue continues.

# MY FATHER'S APOSTROPHE

As the smoke screen cleared
The inherited genetic link
Has been blown out of the water.
The drilled in importance of that tiny fleck
No longer holds any significance.
The orange hair and pale skin
Mottled with freckled patterns;
A thousand dark orange apostrophes
Provide no evidence of missing word.
Beyond three generations the line abruptly ends.
So what's in name;
A capital A
Apostrophe
Capital H
No a to follow the e
One r
No e to follow the n.
Passed down from father to son
And returned to by a widowed daughter
A blank beyond a religious war
And years of enduring
He drove the fastest milk cart in the west.

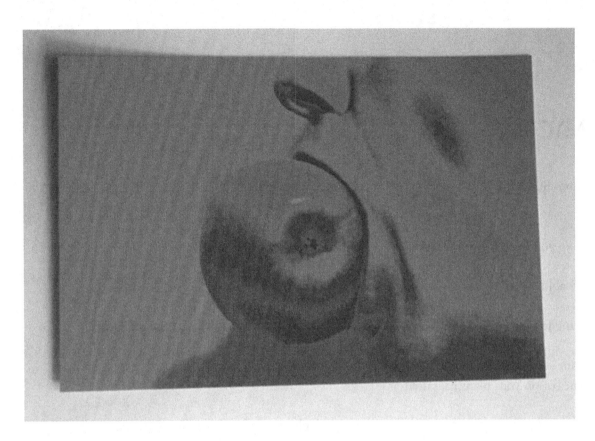

No gagging order command or object
Will silence the voice I have become
As Eve's apple is spewed from my mouth
Here my words wherever you now are
Ideas I had that were above my station
Have provided the steps
Up the long ladder
Freedom is mine
To write and speak
In your silent place
Hope you can hear me now
**<u>My voice is loud</u>**

# MYOPIA

I prevent clarity of vision

                                        Take away results of decisions made.

Trap you in your own situation        Stop visions of what might be.

Disabling you from seeing clearly

                                                          I

bring fog too             far                             off events

I am your lack of foresight
The reason your plans backfire.

                                Failure to see results of your actions
            Your inability to consider what will be.

                                        I am Myopia

and for better or worse

                    You are stuck with me…with me.

# ODE TO FUCK WITT BASTARD!!!

I prefer the term Fuck Witt
But bastard works just as well.
Incompetent supplier and person in delivery van
You can go to fucking hell!

Two days I've waited patiently with fingers crossed
It's now day three of being fucking stuck in.
Maybe the dispatchers a lying bitch
Either way I can't sodding win.

Another bastard delivery van
Passes merrily on its way.
Yet another happy driver tells me
Sorry sweetheart nothing for you today.

LOOK – I've paid my fucking money!!!
REALLY - This just isn't funny!!!
WHERE'S MY PARCEL – YOU FUCKING TWAT!!!
If it comes today
Well I'll eat my fucking hat!!!

# OFF WITH HER HEAD

The trial draws to a close:
However many pure and true,
Drew their conclusions.
"We find the defendant GUILTY"

From behind velvet curtains the Judges,
Pronounced:
"Draw and Quarter her,
Hang by the neck until dead"

The date was set for the next Saturday:
Last entry in her diary read.
'I didn't do it and if I did I didn't know I had.
Punish me if you must.'

On the day:
The crowds jeered and shouted.
Stripped bare,
Not a tear fell.
First cut spilled intestines,
Red and long down her legs.

Outstretched:
Legs and arms bound,
The rope roughly slipped,
Tightly around her neck.
The crowd counted down,
Five! Four! Three! Two! One!

Finally:
With one swift hoist,
She hung high and swung.
Exposed inside and out,
No disputing the guilt in her crimes.

For good measure and security,
They cut her down.
Then took off her head,
And put her in a cardboard box.

# PARTURITION

Procreation is just the beginning
When egg and sperm meet
New creation begins to take form
The creature requires nourishment
Absorbing greedily all it is fed
Then comes pain
Followed by a red show
Water gushes out
Leaving a stain on the carpet
With each stage complete
Pain intensifies
Finally with mucus in its mouth
The being breathes alone
Commanding own identity

The fruit of labour
A new born poem
Wanders into the wilderness
Facing critique and scrutiny
The four legged hairy beast
Walks on two legs
Stands up straight
Moulting as it goes
Revealing its own identity
At first quite ugly
Until inner beauty is explored
Whatever the beast turns into
It is mine and mine alone
Born of love

To share as seen fit
Hiding as required
Words conceived with best intentions
Nurtured and fed on
Emotional intelligence
Don't bully the new creature

Finding its legs
Let it stand alone
This baby is mine
And it will be defended
With might
Don't bully it until it goes away
This creature is my baby
Literary warts and all.

# ...POLKA DOTS...

Once upon a time,
Before lunar bleeding and contractions;
There was a little girl,
In a red polka dot dress
With a fish tail hem.
And lace petticoats that whispered
To shiny red shoes;
Dance like a gypsy,
On the cracked linoleum floor,
Imagine the road yellow.
When lunar bleeding and contractions,
Left her dry and worn;
She realised after half a century,
It was all a polka dot dream,
In plastic shoes,
And polyester petticoats.

# PROLAPSED DEVIL

There is a heavy devil, pulling between my inner thighs;
She has clamped some steel rope, to my gynecological insides.
Every time I sit down, she pulls and she protests;
And with every lie down and stand up, even angrier she gets.
She is very persistent, refusing point blank to go away;
I wish someone would remove her, she has had her day.
All around my pubic mound, in the secret spot of pleasure;
Is a persistent aching pain, variable in measure.
I am on a waiting list, to take the devil away;
But how long exactly is that piece of string, no one can say.

# SILICONE PROTUBERANCES

In a unkempt pub toilet
She lifted her pink sweater
Curious hands copped a feel
Weighed them up.
Those with an egg cup
Talked detail of price
Those with an ample cup
Compared texture and feel.
Back in the 90's
Silicone mammary glands were unheard of
Especially amongst us common folk.

# BOX OF FROGS

There's one for every occasion,
Dull brown and grey pallid ones,
I wonder if maybe their toads.
Many have spectacular bright coloration,
A dazzling array of yellow, green, red and orange,
It seems there are many different varieties,
Living in this box of frogs.

All contained in close confinement,
Sometimes frog venom leaks out,
Cleaning it up is a very dangerous affair.
Once in a blue moon,
When the wind is the right direction,
They franticly leap and jump at the lid,
Trying with all their might to escape.

There have been many attempts to dispose of them,
With the lid fixed on tight with duct tape,
Before depositing them in a park bin,
Or leaving them in the middle of a busy road,
Once I even threw them in a river.
So may futile disposal exercises,
With only disappointment at the end.

Leaving a trail of toxins behind them,
They always find their way home.
Sometimes they can be heard,
Leaping about in a frantic manner.
If someone is nosey and takes off the lid,
They leap all around and escape.

Getting them back in requires much persuasion,
A certain amount of fierce battle,
But always in protective gloves.
So today I throw my box of frogs,
Out and into yet another place,
Invisible frogs in a box,
Now you're off on another a journey.

# PROPHETIC PROSPECT

Restricted, oppressive environment
Forced restraint, unable to move
Intellectual imprisonment
Paralysis brought
From running into brick walls.

Good luck, in better advancement
Important developments
In upside of cycle.
New doors spring open
Releasing
Fortunate turn of events.
A vehicle to drive
Rapid change and new opportunities.

Flexibility required
Juggling, balancing multiple obligations
Splitting resources,
In many directions pulled.
Much jugglery to be done
So it goes
Easy come easy go.

A caring woman
Nurturing queen of emotions.
Choice based on sincere
Sixth sense with artistic creativity,
Prophetic counselling
From a loving friend
Opportunity to turn inward.

A time to rejoice
Joyful, fun occasion
Satisfaction in unity of sharing
Happy hours done for enjoyment,

Freedom from want
Reaping the harvest of labors
Early stage happiness.
Something's coming
Something good.

Striping away worthless matter
Significant life events renewal
Momentous alteration, about to occur,
New era dawning.
All outmoded
To be disregarded,
Transition to rebirth
On horizon
Getting nearer.

# PSEUDONYM RICE

When writing erotic stories and verse
Using your own name can be a curse
To become known as a loose open purse
A nymphomaniac, a tart or worse.

As soon as a writer lets the cat out of the bag
It doesn't automatically make them a slag
A soiled and dirty old washrag
A filthy foul thinking perverted windbag.

When it comes to writing about libido
It's probably best done incognito
As may evidence the presence of a superego
Even Anne wrote under a name no one would know.

So if it's good enough for Howard Allen Francis O'Brien
To be known as Roquelaure and Rampling from time to time
If in breaking the unwritten rules I become pseudonymous
Can I use swear words, write about sex with much less fuss.

If in the future if I publish a book of verse and vice
My alter ego may appear as Suzie Rice
So that when she throws the sexual dice
She will be still Sue whose a bit mad but nice.

Once upon a time, the purpose was clear
Once upon a time, the path was set
Once upon a time, reason was abound
Once upon a time, maybe it's not yet.
Once upon a time, things have been forgotten
Once upon a time, maybe for the best
Once upon a time, life was good
Once upon a time, all was said in jest.
Once upon a time, not that far in the past
Once upon a time, laughter filled the air
Once upon a time, opportunities were vast.
Once upon a time...

# RESPONSE TO PROMPTS TO HONOR ANIMALS

1.  A cat gives birth to a litter.

Just a few months since the last,
Another advert in the free ads.
'Kittens free To Good Home'
Grey runt from last litter
Is now urine scent spraying,
Scrapping Tom, father of many.

2.  The hunter remembers Bambi.

The hunter sits in his Land Rover,
Wiping away tears, he feels foolish,
He's not as macho and ruthless as he thought.
A silent thank-you is said to Walt Disney.
He thinks of his young children at home,
How would they feel if someone shot their mother?

3.  A school of trusting dolphins end up as theme park attraction.

As the star performing attraction, maybe they've forgotten her,
She approached the boat in an effort to communicate her grief.
Captured through her love, she is now part of Waterworld's breeding program.
Watching from her holding tank as her young jump through hoops,
There is little consolation in knowing they will never go hungry or be killed,
The need for freedom to roam the seas the only un-exploitable instinct left.

4.  A bird and squirrel live together like the odd couple.

The first odd couple in the forest; an internet sensation in the making,
The squirrel put his arm around the bird; she sang out and cuddled into his chest.
Twitchers disguised as bushes, immediately posted photos of unlikely couple,
The photos on twitter attracted comments, not possible, must be a Photoshop fake.
The squirrel and the bird the odd couple in the forest,
Opened a bottle of wine, Googled themselves and had a good laugh.

# ROOM OF STORMS

In the room of storms,
Thunder echoes distant drums;
In temptation, lighting gives brief illumination,
To curious animals running for cover.

Propaganda written in stone,
Tells the children;
Galvanise your emotions,
Prepare to be the person once removed.

From somewhere amongst the dunes,
The lone saxophonist;
Plays a warm blue melody,
That touches the shivering heart.

Meanwhile on the other side,
The tide is rising with realisation;
That in the room of storms,
You don't get something for nothing.

For condensed fine vapour,
A silver coin is paid;
No reimbursement given,
For the unfulfilling illumination.

In the room of storms,
Thunder is counted across the sky;
Lightning strikes when it can,
Turning curious animals to carbon.

Leaving the memory,
Of you and I in an embrace;
Under a clear blue sky,
Before we began to ask why.

# SCIENCE AND CREATIVE WRITING

It's often like attempting to read the periodic table,
Many signs and symbols not easily and often never understood.
Electronic configuration and chemical properties,
Have much in common with Microsoft office's spell and grammar check.
To punctuate or not depends on reoccurring trends,
To use the semi colon or not, to add comma's to a list.
Is as understandable as particle physics,
Optimal form and noble gasses.
Elements presented in order of atomic numbers,
Simple words expressed in a complex form.
Still, Professor Brian Cox you keep my interest high,
As does all poets past and present.

# AND MEANWHILE IN SHORT

Things she gave to me
She gave me life
Then took living away
She taught me to claim life for myself.

\*

As the relentless days keep on coming
The shadows cast from no sun
Show only their absence of light.

\*

The story now told many times over again
Has become a lie that guards the truth
A tale that protects the innocent and the guilty.

\*

I told the kids
I'm gonna be Indiana Jones when I grow up
I never managed to do either.

\*

The trouble with experts
They always start corrections with - I Think…
Surely an expert should know.

\*

With a sharp steel pin
POP! She bursts another bubble
Feels empowered and clever
But the stained circle lives on her face forever.

\*

Elizabeth gave me birthday parties
No guests were allowed and there was no cake
Sometimes there was a badge with a number on
The scars from the pin still burns on my chest.

\*

Will you please attempt to speak for me
I seem to of lost my tongue
It wanders with aimless intention.

\*

Watching Channel 4's 'Come Dine With Me'
With a supermarket microwavable value meal on lap
Is somewhat demoralizing.
*

An elastic bandage on my leg
Tablets in stomach creams and potion for unmentionable places
How right to say that age doesn't come alone.
*

Numbers checked and rechecked
Another £2.00 fails to bring results
Twice a week hopes rise before being dashed.
*

A murky and wet start to the day
As we travel through to the evening
More cloud around could be warm and could be cold
Trust me I'm a weather forecaster – not.
*

White paper raises profile
Briefly it's in the day's news bulletin
Results will be resurrected prior to next election.
*

Don't do anything today that's likely to cause a fire
Fire service is on strike
So what is one to do if one is hot stuff.
*

Sorry your knee support that is not quite a calliper
Is no longer available from our medical suppliers
But should the joint break we can fix it on the NHS.
*

Free to good home one woman
Good project in need of repair and restoration
No tax required as age exempts from duty.
*

Twelve weeks on Dermatology waiting list
Twenty one for Neurology
If skin complaint of the brain managed
Maybe could treat as urgent.
*

Handsome curly haired pharmacist
Measured leg for brace
Exposing wobbly chicken leg made face flush
Well that was partly why the red face.
*

Bury us standing up to save room
What's wrong with being upright it was good enough in life
Will the British obsession with being horizontal
Ever die out.
*

Oh Carol you made me a fool
You promised the nation sunshine
When we needed a waterproof kagool.
*

The on button is pushed
It says it wasn't shut down properly
That it needs to update and restart
Me and it have so much in common.
*

Interpret my dreams dear Freudian Psychologist
But bear in mind my brain has holes in it
Be careful in my psyche you may fall through.
*

Contacts list currently unavailable
No Malware detected
Shut down now regularly forced
Through technology I am used.
*

Because I am arrogant enough to have looked death in the face
Politely and firmly declined the invitation to leave
I am doomed to walk between here and there.
*

I really can be unbearably slow
Once it took me three days to write a birthday card
A week to post it and till Xmas to apologize.
*

66

Where once there was a plaster
There's a sticky blackening on my finger
If only I'd pulled it off sooner.

*

To know about quantitative and qualitative surveying is a curse
Oh to read a questionnaire and not imagine results
Not to try and figure out how they will use the survey
To be able to complete forms
In blissful ignorance of their serving purpose.

*

In the subconscious dreaming mind
Involuntary emotions, sensations and ideas
Their content and purpose a mystery to the conscious self
Being left with that was it a dream or reality feeling
Is so frustrating but maybe I dreamt that.

*

Hey cognitive behavior therapist
Running through a film in life's theatre hasn't worked
Shall we give meridian tapping a go?

*

When writing in erotic verse
Use of Nome de plume is advised
Sex verse like sex itself works better incognito.

*

Loud snoring and copulation do not make for good bedfellows
A buddy of a certain ilk that fulfils a need
Is of no use if they leave before the morning awakenings.

*

When your firm parts start to loosen and head for ankles
Don't bother wearing tight elasticized padded underwear
That just sends a fake message that leads to disappointment
Let things swing like a badge of honor and emblem of experience.

*

Dubito cogito ergo sum
A lesson from their Mum
Borrowed from Rene Descartes
And used to impress at dinner parties.

*

When we win millions on the lottery
We're gonna buy a beach and live in a cave
Live without other people technology and stuff
Apart from an internet connection to buy shopping
And a car in case we suddenly need to escape
Oh and register at a doctors in case we're ill
Maybe this idea needs rethinking.

*

I am a self-confessed Christmas dodger
Religion and Capitalism combined
Is best avoided.

*

Oh Karen, my secrets and you
All rolled up together
There is nothing we can do
To get ourselves together
We are trapped knee deep in poo.

*

To pay my bills and get discount I need an internet connection
To get an internet connection I need to get a contract
To make sure I don't get robbed or infected I need an ant virus
To avoid further charges I need to register for paper free billing
To live without the internet costs
To live with the internet costs.

*

# SILVER GODDESS

Without her I am nothing
Note even a tiny sparkle.
Without her my silver soul
Would be black.

Without her
There would be no love songs.
No mention of lovers
Secret meetings.

Without her
There would be no tide.
No ebb and flow
No day and night.

Without her
There would be no tide to take out.
Without her planets would wither
Without her I have no purpose.

For the sake of smelling nice
Getting to a destination with ease.
Do not abandon her
Without her you to will have no point.

# SNOEM

A release of all bodily tensions
Brings a comforting warmth,
A distant unfocussed smile
Waits to erupt
Like the child anticipating snow.

Words fall like flakes from the sky
Some melt and disappear into rivers
Whilst others are captured and frozen in time.
Converted from crisp white too black Times New Roman
Whistling and a humming their song.

In the galaxy of putting consonants and vowels
Into abstract shapes and concrete forms,
Representations of sounds
Stretch their legs in wide open stance,
Expressing welcome enjoyment of the senses portrayed.

In a relaxed posture the air of readiness
Verbalizes the pros and the cons,
Brings licking the lips with cautious hope
An upturned face with sparkling eyes
And eyebrows rising in pleasant amusement.

A playful pinch nudge and a warm cuddle
In the natural tendency to form words
That flurry onto the clean page,
Poetic water vapor like the morning mist in the atmosphere
Becomes suspended on pulped wood; cloth or fiber for all time.

# TATTLETALE TANGO

In a terpsichorean hold
A dramaturge devours the floor,
Tension is high and tight;
As unwitting partners are held,
Within a tight firm hold.

Movements of camaraderie
Crackle with static energy,
Sparking off every step taken;
Both in and out of hold,
The dance promises legitimacy.

Tattletale Tango steps
As the tergiversate illustrates,
Works equally as well;
From near and far,
Both in and out of hold.

# TAXI

Seen these sights over and over again,
done the same things not diverting from old routine.
Rather than call a taxi when one is needed
better to be early than late a habit hard to break,
whilst the person I am meeting is inevitably late.
On balance being born was the first problem
and then it really just went from there.

The first to be removed was the waiting area
along with incubation tank.
The second tried to leave of own accord
just made a ruptured break for it.
The third a scrapping of lichen
taken from the trunk.
Now another waiting period,
will more parts of the whole need to be removed?
Or is the taxi to my last appointment
going to take me to a final destination?

# THE GRAND OLD DAME OF YORK

(To the tune of The Grand Old Duke of York)

Oh the grand old dame of York
She had a few thousand men
She marched them up the wooden hill
And she marched them down again
And when they were up she'd fuck
And when they were down she'd frown
And when they were only half way up
They'd been out on the town.

# THE PLAYERS

*They tell me:*
Sun shines in through one
Out the other.

*I tell them:*
My orifices and omissions
Are my concern.

*They whisper:*
She's not very green
But is cabbage looking.

*Director shouts:*
Roll camera
Action!

*The cast say:*
We are a play
On your stage.

*I tell them:*
Body language only
Indicates the end.

*Credits role:*
Them – *starring as they*
Me – *starring as I*
The cast – *starring as themselves*

Director – *supreme nameless entity*

# THE WEATHER GIRL, WELLIES AND ME

In preparation for what might be to come
A flick of the switch
Allows entry into my personal space.
The juxtaposition of what she is saying
Wrestles with her overall appearance.

With beautiful coiffured hair,
Perfect flawless eyes, lips and skin.
Patterned with bright flowers in bloom
Her short sleeveless dress reveals
What is likely an all over tan.

Out of that mouth with perfect white teeth
Spews foul language of the day.
The girl in the summer frock, skin tanned golden brown
Talks of damage, deluge, torrents,
Saturation, high winds, flooding and risk

As the run off causes surface water
Her advice is be very cautious.
She says gusting winds are picking up
But let's focus on the rain for now,
Remember you can always ring the flood line if concerned

Surface water will be potentially disruptive
Amber flood warnings are out in many places.
The beauty in summer attire say's; it's not looking good,
The next few days won't be great at all,
We could even see the appearance of frost.

Totally disgruntled
With both the forecast and presenter
I turn off the switch
Removing her from my home
I'm gonna do this the old fashioned way.

On opening the curtains
A bright blue sky is revealed
The ground is a bit wet
But not a rain cloud in sight
Trust the weather girl, my ass.

No raincoat and wellies needed
Just a jacket and some pumps.
I partake in the morning walk to the shop.
Halfway there the heavens opened soaking me to the bone,
Loathing grows on thinking she was right.

Like a drowned rat
I sulk all the way home.
At least I'm not in a short summer frock
Leaving puddles of fake tan as I go.
Weather girl I hate you more now coz you were right.

In my head I hear,
Today's weather, brought to you by mucus cough syrup.
Now donning a long rain coat, wellies and a hat
I've added mucus cough syrup to my shopping list.
Coz knowing my luck, she'll be right about needing that.

The moral is
If it looks too good to be true
Maybe it isn't.
This is not always the case
But over a short summer dress
Always wear a waterproof Mac.

# THIS IS WHAT SHE SAID

All the things she said,
Not said well enough to spur action.
Things she said,
Transferred into learning by rote.
Just like the child,
Who learned to clean their teeth.
Without the prompt,
Of what she said.
This is what she said,
Get up,
Get ready,
Wear a coat,
Get a move one.
The conditioned response,
To everything she said.
This is what she,
The cat's mother said.
Thanks Mam.

# TO CALL FROM BEHIND THE WALL

To lead
To check
To think
To see

My nature is to lead with suspicion,
Any gift horse checked for fleas.
There's always more to what I'm thinking,
More than what you think you see.

Call for deeds, from truth
Equality

Dark times often call for dark deeds,
In light being softly faithful and true.
The black swan glides behind equally as far,
The white swan leads forward bravely.

Without defences
Weapons
Actions
Things

Do you come with painful weapons?
Intent to injure without care?
If so beware
Things are not always what they seem
My strength is a secret weapon of choice.

Often in frustration
Often with pain
...kindness,
Fright.

Painful is bearable at a cost,
Kindness as the breaker.
Everyone has something worth fighting for,
The costs not always first agreed.

Having relief
Having action
Having freedom
Having change

Have you come to injure or relieve?
Actions given time will tell all, reveal.
I feel the change, it is a coming,
Time blows freely through my hair.
Timely waiting
Timely close
Timely right
Time out

Time spent waiting behind an impenetrable wall,
Gate keys close at hand.
Waiting for signals to be given,
To open and peer out.

To call freely
To communicate often
Have choice
Possess time
Feel free
To hold, eternally
Be equal
Be brave

To not be anxious
…alone
…not without
Timid, scarred
Wanting
To not be contradictory
Be conflicting

To call freely and walk out
To leave behind the wall
To acknowledge the signals
To cast off restrictions
To move with freedom
To be honest and open
To speak openly
To be too…

# TURRETS SECRETS

There's a turret atop the castle with no windows or sun
The stone stairwell is pitted narrow and long
Where moss forms random patterns on damp dark stone
Lights flicker as decayed worn wires fail to hold their power

Observing those who attempt the climb
Mottled faded daguerreotypes whose history is long lost
Stare down with weary sepia eyes

Few regal suitors charming in their manner
Have attempted admission to the turret's room
A solid door securely fastened

Impenetrable locks and bolts deny entry
Not clenched angered fist nor tender loving kindness
Can persuade the door to fall open

On a rare occasion a confident suitor tries and fails
In attempting the journey alone into the unknown
To gain access to the room at the top of the turret
That holds secrets behind the eyes.

# UNTITLED

When stepping out of darkness adds illumination to hidden pain
Shadows creep across the heart,
Dense cloud fogs any gain.

In attempted honesty as events are recalled,
Lies hope of liberation.
Survival in conversations breath,
A hopeful form of reconciliation.
Fine-tuned words as truth attempted gives little to no consolation.

Black holes prevent hurtful recalling,
Each trapped in own coping strategy.
When sorry words and actions do nothing but fall as senseless flattery.
Nothing can explain or condone,
Wasted actions of patriarchy.

Only slight in healing and worsening in hurt through the onslaught of time
Know this lights of my life, blame is not yours it's completely and absolutely mine.

# UNUTTERED WAVES

The tide can be gentle or earth moving
High with foaming waves or soft and quietly moving
Either way it's natural.

Oh yes, it's a natural release,
Running through course sand into the surf
Great salt waves crashing onto legs
And leaving white salt stains in its wake.
Sensual rolling tide flowing in and out
Many feel the need, whilst some abstain completely.

Walking the tide alone
And never admitting to taking the stroll,
Not an outspoken public event
Knowing others go there can ease guilty conscience.

# VULVARLY UNFAMILIAR SIGHT

Has it changed in shape and size?
Is it a different color?
How'd I know?
It's not like I hold it when I pee,
I don't hold it my hand in the shower
And think wow that's a whopper,
Or arrange it in my underpants.

Straddle a mirror and acquaint yourself,
Apparently one is never too old for familiarization
With the secret lady garden.
I know what it's called,
What it feels like,
What it's for,
As for what mine personally looks like
Honestly I'm more familiar with my nose.

If it committed a crime or was stolen
I couldn't point to a line up and say,
Yep, that one's definitely mine.

# W MALARKEY

With this writing lark comes so many questions, so many W words.

Why have you used that phrase?
*Coz it fits.*

What is it all about?
*Anything you like.*

Where's it all leading to?
*Somewhere and nowhere.*

Will they ever be published?
*Simple answer is I don't know.*

When did you write this and that?
*Mostly I can't remember.*

What if no one likes them?
*Not that bothered.*

Would you write one about me?
*Possibly, at some point.*

Wonder if this refers to that event?
*It refers to anything you want.*

Words don't make sense, why?
*That's just how it is.*

Whatever on earth is that all about?
*Can't explain, don't want to.*

Writing poetry isn't that hard, is it?
*Try it and see for yourself.*

Were you always a writer?
*Guess so, hopefully I still am.*

Who influences you?
*Everyone.*

What influences you?
*Everything.*

I suppose the short answer to all the W questions malarkey is, whatever.

# WAVE GIVING YOU

Your final journey began on the Celtic and North Sea
Followed by a short trip down the Great Western Union
You travelled down the Thames in Oxford
Stopped off in London before heading out into the English Channel.

On the second leg of your journey
Art design and media waved you off from Murano
And the venetians said a prayer
Graphic Designers cried as you sailed off into the Med.

Customer officers speaking in tongues, foreign and of faith
Checked you for narcotics before stamping you clear to go in
Others fearing you contagious waved you through in haste.

America refused you entry no visa allowed for you
Australia and New Zealand welcomed you in
Where you sailed away across the Tasmanian Sea.

So many countries welcomed you
And prayed to their different Gods
That the final leg of your journey would be better than any before.

From many a country you set sail on a journey that can only be made alone;
Saudi Arabia, Cuba, India, Russia, South Africa and many more.
In Japan English language learners
Said prayers in their Mother tongue
Buddhist monks in Pusan lit candles in paper boats
To help guide you on your way.

Every instructed detail of your last journey carried out in full
Together we visited the world
I left a small piece of you behind in water as instructed
Now every time I see the sea
You give me a wave just as you wanted.

# WHIPPET WALKER

Once I met a man on a blind date
Who said he was fond of walking his whippet,
Having no urge to walk his whippet for him,
We agreed I wasn't his type.

# WINTER

With my beautiful silver transparent wings,
At first I glide gently and slowly in.
Brining with me the shortness of day,
Extending the darkness of night.
Moving air quickly with my natural force,
Trees sway to resist me.
A fight lost to the prevailing of my wind.

Branches whisper to nature's growth,
It's about to happen soon.
Although exactly when is unknown,
But the series of events has begun.
The cause of important changes,
Nestled in between autumn and spring.
I am winter feel the chill in speaking my name.

Sometimes mild most often severe,
Harsh, wet and cold.
Birds have left to avoid my language,
I can and will, kill and destroy.
The very old and the brand new are first to respond,
As I bring with me, hypothermia, novo virus, hunger,
Seasonal depression, rain and black ice.

The back story is more purposeful,
Holding the real need for my existence.
I have poetic justice at my disposal,
The ironic twist of fate dealt by nature's players.
I am the allegory that is winter,
Lengthening with every passing year.
My beauty destroys, aids and envelopes all.

Through my harsh famine months,
Communities huddle in uncertainty of their survival.
Starvation not an uncommon event.
I will cover you,
With my beautiful silver transparent wings.
Until astronomical events are evidenced,
In the mating of animals and tiny green shoots.

Through the time when the sun on the horizon,
Appears at its low altitude.
Calendar based methods cannot pin me down,
Nature herself has lost control over me.
The appearance of green buds and crocus,
No longer mark the end of my arrest.
In deception calm and warmth are felt.


Feel the downdraft of my silver wings,
As I swoop with an unexpected second attack.
I am the beautiful bird of winter,
Bringing a wonderland on my wings.
Glistening with silver sparkles,
Against the beautiful red sky at dawn,
Giving you fair warning.

My beauty sparkles,
But my voice is cruel.
Hear me roar in the pouring rain,
Listen to me moan in the whispering trees.
Feel me bite through your coat,
Hurting your delicate skin.
You will not forget the pain of my beauty
As I take you under my beautiful silver transparent wings.

# WAITING TO BE ASSESSED.

In the red brick building,
Where doors are locked and minds are broken.
The sign above stubbed out cigarette ends declares,
No Smoking in or outside of this building.
Cover of Chat magazine on the waiting room table reads,
Raped For 50p and a Biscuit.
A red sign with white capital letters warns
CAUTION STEP BEHIND DOOR.
In the corridor heavy footsteps pass,
And electronics whir and hum to a different tune.
Behind a locked green door,
Muffled voices make life saving decisions.
From under a hooded coat a frightened woman measures,
The distance from waiting room to out the front doors.
The hot radiators with flaking paint offer no warmth,
Locked windows offer no fresh air.
The wait to sort out the real from the imagined,
Continues into the longest of times.

In the place for emergencies,
Where there is waiting behind a red line.
Stop it or cop it, abuse will not be tolerated,
Just because it's legal doesn't make it safe,
Staff are not responsible for, loss or theft of property.
Stop, think, and choose well…
Let's talk, let us know what you think, good or bad?
You're dehydrated, Refresh yourself, Beat the thirst.
Are you a dream boyfriend by day, and a control freak by night.
You wouldn't call the coastguard if you fell in a puddle,
Not an emergency, stop, think…
Do you really need 999.
And someone else is sleeping rough tonight.

And the signs say there are no directions,
Sit and wait where you now are.

91

# WORDS OF ICE.

In a perpetual winter of words of ice,
        The bough has broken,
        Letting the cradle fall.

Leaving anger and sadness hanging
From irreparable broken branches.

        Words of ice weigh heavy,
        Dragging down too decay;
        Splintered fragments of the tree.

No amount of warmth can revive
        The hot air turned ice.
        New seeds planted,
        Die before germination;
With no potential against cold.

        The breath of a cold sharp axe
        Ensures an unhappy ending.

In a perpetual winter of words of ice;
        There are only so many times,
        The tree might take revival.

# WORDSWORTH'S SISTER

In search for Dorothy I was offered;
Low prices and free delivery in the UK
Latest summer '13 collections from somewhere.co.uk
Links to breast enhancement, body fillers and scrubs.
Review of matches at Harmony
Cookie detectives must have reported to Mr Y A Hoo
That search was done by a lonely old woman in need.

Great controller of cyber space let's get one thing fucking straight,
I don't want to buy the sodding book I just want to know who she was,
I am not in need of a skirt to hide my hips, my arse is flat ok!
I'm happy with my tits, thighs, nose and wrinkles,
Life experience tells Harmony should be fuck your life up good and proprer.com.
Too much advertising pushes push pushing.

Antivirus flagged links to Dorothy with suspicion and warns caution,
Does Mr MCA Fee know more than he's letting on?
Local librarian said no nothing on their shelves,
Would I like to use a computer to search again online?
For the time being Dorothy you will have to remain
Wordsworth's sister.

# THE MACHINE IS NOW WELL OILED.

The machine is now well oiled,
At long last, released from quarantine;
And out from the back of the cupboard.

I have sweated and I've toiled,
In making it shiny and clean;
The machine is now well oiled.

In the madness there is method,
In getting the cogs mobile and seen;
And out from the back of the cupboard.

I'm now prepared to cut the mustard,
Bang loudly on my tambourine;
The machine is now well oiled.

My emotions are displayed un-awkward,
On show in a solid oak vitrine;
And out from the back of the cupboard.

All polishing and cleaning for this dullard,
Worthwhile it most certainly has been;
The machine is now well oiled,
And out from the back of the cupboard.

# EMMA, WHERE'S MY JACKET?

The night is black, as clouds separate Venus and Mars,
A lone wolf marks with scent Seaman's Mission walls.
High on his haunches, he stalks and calls,
With jaws to the sky and neck outstretched,
Eaaaa-maaa, Emma, Emmmmm, Eaaaaaa-maaaaa;
Sending his love Lorne howl, Emmmmmaaaa…
Bouncing out over Mannheim Quay,
Across sails and mast and through the archway,
Into the courtyard where Emma was last seen.
Em, Emmmmm, Eamma, Emma,
Whhhhhere are youuuuuu?
The wolf, fleet of foot, howls out his message;
Emma, Emm, Emma, Emmmmmmmmaaaaaa,
Whhhhhere'sssss my jaaaaacket?
Emmaaaaaaa
Where are you?
His persistent desperate howling,
Gave Emma second thoughts;
As the clouds clear between Venus and Mars,
The Wolf, Emma and the jacket;
Are reunited and silence falls.

# EFFERVESCENT KARMA.

Miscellaneous necessary equations
Form sum of whole parts;
A consequential path prompts
Inconsequential speech.

Words spoken out of turn,
Momentarily disrupt momentum;
Briefly disrupting audaciousness
Of imaginative resources.

Destabilizing magic spell
With condemnation;
The blaggard's faces grin,
Prompting a surprised expression.

Frequency disturbance
Brought white noise;
Entering the psyche
Momentarily breaking the sequence.

Placebo affect acquired
Synergy and harmony returned;
Effervescence bubbles on
Multiplying in intensity.

Spontaneity smiles broadly
Disparate capitulation departs;
Peacefully karma is restored,
To flow unreservedly without restraint.

# A…PHOBIA

Fear, the price of a vivid imagination;
Feeds short burst anxiety trigger,
It is the hand on a counterfeit gun

Emotional intelligence, an undesired gift;
Pours salt into angry wounds,
Self-devouring ravenous isolation
Induces loneliness and consumes equilibrium.

Obligation, a staggering responsibility
Lays concealed under a woolen blanket.

Time, past the hour to the hour;
Prompts the savant
Proceed with caution

Askance eyes, reflect no trust
Only all-consuming suspicion and doubt.

Atavistic instinct arguably elevates behavior;
Combines flight and fight confusion
Liquefying the concrete world.

It runs in streams down the walls
Feeding the tigers thirst
As the tail burns palms.

# BEST POLICY HOTEL.

In the hotel of immediate reaction and consequences,
the boardroom is filled to capacity.
For the sake of the few at the top table,
sacrifices will be made.
Vicious campaigners converge in great number;
various options are up for consideration.
According to their glory seeking principles,
the answer lies in grief and semi-permanent rapport.
Halfway between rehabilitation and real time,
makes for better results and allows failures to be ignored.
Parts creating the whole are shaved to fit,
until slices of the pie form a perfect circumference.
The semi-functional illiterate with their conditioned responses,
form further committees to make irrelevant decisions.
Those who did not take the stairs of learning,
travel in the lift straight to the roof.
Where assumptions take on concrete form,
through inaccurate minutes with signatures at the end.
Actions to be evidenced on completion,
filter down from floor to floor to lobby.
Where the inexperienced and ambitious few,
interpret and redesign the notes to satisfy their own ends.
In the hotel of immediate reaction and consequences,
temporary quick fix gut reactions make for best policy.

# ANTISEPTIC

There is a part of me,
Only visible in your presence;
We are like two sides
Of the same spinning coin,
Alternating between heads and tails.

When the hand of fate flicks a thumb,
Flips us way up high;
There is no way of knowing
Which of us if either,
Will land on the upside.

Our disdainful heritage,
Galvanizes a joint destiny;
As the sins of the parents
With each rejecting gesture,
Are passed along the line.

Ammunition is plentiful,
Ricocheting back and forth;
Piercing already weekend resolve
Leaving dried crusts of blood,
Hidden by artificial language.

Accept my offer of peace,
Antiseptic saturated gestures;
Band-Aids for our wounds
To heal in forgiveness,
With the offering of a hand.

This is a part of me, just here,
Only viable in your acceptance;
We are two sides of the same coin,
Spinning, spinning … …
Trapped in midair.

# ROLLOVER PRAYER

Oh dear Lord won't you send me
A rollover lottery win,
So I can improve things
And were a great big grin.

I promise to give to charity
Be generous where I can,
And not fritter it away
Getting an all over winter tan.

If you do this for me Lord
I promise I'll be good,
And feed starving people
Living without food.

And when my time comes
And I'm in the queue for hell,
I can afford to strike a bargain
With the Devil as well.

# MAGMA

Sometimes small things falling through the cracks,
End up giving a whole heap of pain.
What you running from in such a hurry,
Slow down, take some deep breaths and relax a while.
I'm not exposing mine, not until I see yours.
Well I conceded and showed mine,
In return you backed off.

I'm not looking for something very serious,
No twitchy awkward contact
Just some small friendly sharing,
A bit of this, for a bit of that.
Those small things,
They've fallen through the cracks
Now they're fit to burst.

A volcano is ready to erupt.
Creatures of fantasy strike the pose,
When finally it blows up high
They'll be as real as you and me.
Maybe I'm being way to cynical,
Is that encouragement or neglect
In your eyes.

Ease of manner and cautious curiosity
Meets confident shinny star chaser,
Comes up against self-reliance
Rubbing shoulders with independence.
That's a whole lot of red magma
Just waiting to blow.
Then again maybe I'm too suspicious by half.

# AFTER ALL

### 1)  All in All

Pitch black slander,
taken as truth,
at face value.
No favors owed,
makes us even.
Consolidation needed.
Not retribution.
Ice broken,
past reconciled,
in apology,
lies no shame.
Sorry in words,
forgiveness in actions.

### 2)  All's Well.

Cards on table,
transparency by degrees.
Brings elephant back,
filling empty space,
dominating the room.
Fossilized terms,
meticulously regurgitated,
reveal catalogue of hurt.
In flaming anger,
spewed out loud.
Monkeys here now,
clinging securely,
to our backs.

3) All's Ill.

There's no quelling,
defeat accepted,
sorry not enough.
Illusionary devises fail.
Keystone falls broken,
bringing rubble down.
Too much hatred,
Too much war damage.
Induces action,
defeat conceded,
walk away,
live to fight,
another day.

4) All's Mine.

This is yours,
that's mine,
sorting out starts.
In uncomfortable silence,
amicably respecting space,
division begins.
Ownership dispute erupts,
turning to sour grapes.
Who did what to who,
what was said,
dredge up black slander.
No blood spilled,
Just ego bruised.

5)  All Over.

Inheritance broken,
Photos torn in two.
Without laying of hand,
internal bruises,
reignite fire.
Inflammable dialogue,
Evidences conclusion.
Car loaded,
one suitcase,
music collection,
box of broken dishes.
No fond farewell,
just relief.

6)  All that's left

Another experience,
Intense discomfort,
Disillusion,
Furious disappointment,
Disquiet in heart.
Empty bed,
Meals for one,
Freedom.
To grasp,
Enjoy,
Start again,
Chalk up experience.
All's well in the end.

# I WANNA HAVE A HIT SINGLE ;-)
# THIS IS NOT A LOVE SONG.

As the bus drove past I thought shit,
I missed it what do I do now.
Then realized I'm not even waiting for a bus.
So I sat on a bench,
Feet surrounded by empty beer cans.
I thought, I'm gonna have a hit single,
And so I wrote one, I mean how hard can it be.
Well I've got the beginning, I've got a start.

Oh yes, looks like I'm gonna be famous.

Sounding good so far, I'm into the second verse,
Without a single mention of crying.
Not a hint of heart break and woe,
No sobbing and words full of poor me.
I'm so lonely please come back home.
This is easier than I thought it would be.
This hit single things dead easy,
Got myself a cash cow here.

Cool, looks like I'm gonna be rich.

I put my note book in my pocket,
Gonna write the music when I get home.
Beep beep- beep beep,
Check my text messages,
Oh no it says I've been dumped.
Is that good or bad, never cared much anyway.
Memo to self, don't write an I've been dumped song.
Hello, do you know when the next bus is, said the smiling face.

Looks like my next projects gonna be a love song.

Never did get around to writing that love song,
Though I put pen to paper many times.
There was the marriage certificate,
The mortgage agreement and bridging loan,
Consent forms for kid's school trips.
I wrote loads of sex me up emails,
All used as evidence in the divorce.
The smiling face won't speak to me anymore.

Who needs love?
I'm gonna have a hit single.

# VENTILATION VS FOUNDATION

The ordinary gentleman wears a leather jacket and Chinos,
He likes the wicked ventilation of not wearing underwear.
Hidden by leather brogues his cracked hard skin bleeds.
In his pocket alongside his calf skin wallet,
He carries an i-phone he doesn't fully know how to use,
If only he could work out how to use the apps,
He could chat with his 648 friends on Facebook,
Even though he has never met 640 of them,
He is comforted by such a high number.
At home in the evening after his steak and chips,
He has another go at mastering the Sky+ box,
Gives up and returns to Freeview.

VS

The ordinary lady wears a Monsoon coat,
With Per Una slacks and sweater.
Foundation garments hold loose flesh firm,
While her sling back wedgies hurt her feet.
In her fake Prada handbag she evidences her status,
A purse full of plastic and Chanel makeup.
Her mobile is a basic model for emergencies only,
She Skype's her friends and family from home.
Social networking sites are not for her,
The fear of hackers has put her right off.
Her meals consist of locally sourced organic produce,
No horsemeat in her shopping trolley.

These two should get together, work out technological stresses in harmony,
Share likes and dislikes,
Compare the disadvantage and advantage of wearing foundation underwear and none,
Spend hours debating
Skype vs Facebook
Horsemeat vs Organic
Ventilation vs Foundation.

# WTF

Somewhere out there
In the city tonight,
Perfectionists' role over
Give up the fight.
Save the grammar
Had no luck,
Academics muster resources
And say WTF.

afaik
Some cry let the battle commence
With Tennyson's Light Brigade,
Others cry and stamp their feet
As written words
For better or worse transform.

0.5 a lege 0.5 a lege
0.5 a lege onwrd
all in2 valy o dth
rd 600
4wd lite brgde
chrg 4 gns e sd
in2 valy o dth
rd 600.

fyi imho
4 im a br of vry ltl brain
& wds bthr me
gg gg uk 4 a gg
lemntry my dr watsn
Should be read
In grammatical entirety.
coz tomoz
u b soz
When the eloquence of words
Are reduced
To a meagre sms text.

# 165 MILES WITH EXTRA CARE

The old broken suitcase is filled to bulging
With prodigious bulk and worn out shoes;
Whilst in the background the subconscious
Resembling a string bag, prattles away.
Tragedies mask fits where it touches
Squeezing in all the wrong places,
Threatening to drop and leave bewildered disappointment.
Please clinical moronisim, give me a break,
Oh please, 007-ish reactions don't leave me now.

It's hard not to think this way,
Whilst about to meander, eyes partially open,
Into a dalliance and deferral
With officialdom and inefficient bureaucracy.
With its administrative systems
And non-specific departments,
Run by academically challenged pen pushers.

I have created a picture of her
Trying to read my case file;
Armed with her posthumous title
Reduced to the acronym ECC,
Probably given as an incentive
To counteract low pay scale.

So I sit on the old suitcase,
Looking at packing cases waiting to be filled
With fifty four years of life;
Staring at the phone,
Willing the Extra Care Coordinator
To live up to her title and tell me,
The first step on the 165 mile journey
Starts today.

# A SILENT VILLANELLE

In this, a culture of conquer by division,
The loudest whispers try to say;
We've been beaten into submission.

Divided into, intimidated nonparticipation,
We go about hushed business, day by day;
In this, a culture of conquer by division.

With extra care, placed in every intonation,
Having unwittingly become actors in a play;
We've been beaten into submission.

Successful in their noisy fragmentation,
Rules are, you want to play you'll pay;
In this, a culture of conquer by division.

Whilst they revel, in their own glorification,
Of our way, no way or the highway;
We've been beaten into submission.

Still we conform to the master's vision,
As we tiptoe quietly, through each day.
In this, a culture of conquer by division,
We've been beaten into submission.

# AUDACITY OF HOPE

That thing that's not just a number until
beyond the first legal taste of alcohol,
and at the other end when a physician says;
well at your age that's to be expected.

Dementia is just the realization,
that one can no longer be doing with the audacity of hope;
creased and struggling to get out of the chair,
a walking cane in the last lesion of life,
bearing the weight of the fanciful implementation of time.

Perceptual facts ricochet through the upper skull,
confused by the present participle,
in a future that looks tense.

So typically unreasonable of the grand plotter of things,
to give the audacity of hope,
just in time for being beyond caring.

# TOPOLOGICAL SHOES

Wearing tightly woven
Ill fitting,
Unsuitable
Topological shoes;
No matter the topology,
Through holes in the soles
Blisters of emotional connections. . .
Rub and bleed out.
Canvas substrate,
Lacks environmental strength
On redoubtable terrain;
Formidable footwear
Is the directive.

# CONVENIENTLY DEAD

Conveniently dead, doesn't mean you're excused,
From your secret occupation;
Of what you did to those you used.

Marks are left, on those you branded,
With your diseased violation;
Conveniently dead, doesn't mean you're excused.

Still remaining, the walking wounded,
With nothing left to the imagination;
Of what you did to those you used.

With actions, still not comprehended,
Of the persistent and lingering humiliation;
Conveniently dead, doesn't mean you're excused.

In death, the crimes remain unanswered,
No opportunity for confrontation;
Of what you did to those you used.

Of all the crimes, unnamed and unnumbered,
The worse is death giving disassociation.
Conveniently dead, doesn't mean you're excused,
Of what you did to those you used.

# HISTORIC OOZE.

They call it historic,
Like an old book from the top shelf;
With the dust blown off,
Landing on the skin of those looking to see.

Indian ink leaves the pages,
Becoming a mark on the author,
A brand never completely removed;
Ghosts from the past,
Rejoice at being released,
As every page screams,
Live with us we are you.

From the dark of the coal shed,
Into the bed at night,
And out into the light of day;
With every attempt at empathy,
Received as sympathy,
The branding iron burns.

There is neither excuse nor pardoning,
For being the victim,
Or committing the crime;
Once the scars are reopened,
And poison begins to ooze,
There is no turning back.

# I'M NOT READY TO LET GO COMPLETELY.

I'm losing the ability to read,
I am widowed yet again.
How can you write this?
I hear your question.
I can write in a somewhat dysfunctional automatic mode,
In the same way one knows to put food in one's mouth.
I can now only read a very small amount;
A very short poem,
A newspaper headline
And the opening paragraph.

I keep buying books;
And travel through the disappointment
Of not being able to get past one or two pages,
Not remembering what I have just read.
And then comes the overwhelming dryness,
Tearless grief that the ability to enjoy a book
Is gone.

My academic skills,
What remains of them;
Now relies on implicit memory
And even that is deteriorating.
I cannot remember the form of a Villanelle,
Now each time I write one
It involves hours of looking at the format,
Relooking and relooking,
Simplifying and note taking.

Poetry is becoming too much of chore,
But I cling to what is evidence
Of once having had an academic and creative mind.

My Occupational Therapist and Neuropsychologist,
Have both suggested I abandon;
Poetic form and structure
Grammar
Punctuation
And spelling.
They say I should maybe try and write
A series of poems in my own way;
A collection written by me as I am now,
I suspect they have left out -before it goes completely.

I don't think I'm ready yet,
To let go completely.
I have stopped buying newspapers;
The TES and TLS,
The Observer, Times and Guardian.
I no longer buy books,
My Kindle just gathers dust.

But I still have a little hope left
And until that leaves,
I will continue trying and failing.

When the last of what is left of my
Academic and creative skills are gone;
Who will I be?
I am not quite ready to be
Absolutely no-one,
Not just yet.

# INVOLUNTARY OBTUSNESS

The bigger problem of just being,
Keeps getting bigger.
All modes of keepsakes have been exhausted:
Spontaneity, Contemplation,
Reflection, Abstention,
Buddhism, Wiccan,
Asatru, to some extent Atheism,
Faithful involuntary obtuseness,
Remains locked in the inability to concentrate;
Hovering like a Mayfly,
Might-fly, Could-fly,
Can't possibly-fly,
If only the right vehicle were to announce itself
And prevent rolling over.

Binoculars are out of focus,
The distance horizon-less
And the near a faraway place;
Reading letters off the opticians card
Has become a unilateral bifocal affair,
Within a sepia time lapsed film
Projected onto an old stone wall,
Speeding up
Slowing... down,
In glorious surround sound
As silent as the movie itself,
With a pregnant interlude
The grainy footage illustrates involuntary obtuseness,
Of the bigger problem
Of just being.

# SITTING PRECARIOUSLY

Sitting precariously, on the in-between fence,
Observing life's tide, coming in high going out low;
Wishing in the moonlight for clairvoyance.

There's been a test, of will and patience,
All lined up, yesterday's heroes, friend and foe;
Sitting precariously, on the in-between fence.

The one most disturbing, in the past tense,
Is the one mumbling, stay, no go on, go on;
Wishing in the moonlight for clairvoyance.

For an interlude, in the deafening silence,
Just once more to have a chattering rainbow;
Sitting precariously, on the in-between fence.

Waiting for a break, a lift in the suspense,
As ever and always, in the quiet ditto, ditto;
Wishing in the moonlight for clairvoyance.

And you may say, in this first instance,
Jump down, don't be the lonely fellow;
Sitting precariously, on the in-between fence,
Wishing in the moonlight for clairvoyance.

# WRONG CHOICE OF EMBROCATION

The peripheral voice shouts, choose!
Having moved in more centrally;
You made the wrong choice, you lose.

Time has come to sensibly peruse,
That for which you're blameworthy;
The peripheral voice shouts, choose!

This is not a deceptive ruse,
For you there is no amnesty;
You made the wrong choice, you lose.

All you do is further contuse,
When relating words of sympathy;
The peripheral voice shouts, choose!

Witch-hazel won't heal the bruise,
The past weighs to heavy:
You made the wrong choice, you lose.

The poison continues to ooze,
From a painfully unbearable bruise.
The peripheral voice shouts, choose!
You made the wrong choice, you lose.

# BREEDING COBRAS AN UNINTENDED CONSEQUENCE

In trying to attain a desired effect
an unexpected determent occurred.
In efforts to give the sunny side
a black cloud descended and settled.
In contradiction to original intentions
it is believed I am breeding Cobras.
In giving gifts meant to show love
the intention was support not purchase.
In unintentional,
unanticipated,
unforeseen consequences,
I see why you dub me a snake.
In what was thought best intentions
I have become the law of unintended consequence.
In misguided means to give you it all
I have given you unintended consequences.

# IDIOTM

Shilly shallying backroom boys and girls
Erring on the side of angels
Draw in their horns.

An upset apple cart plain as day
Now filled with sour grapes
Pulled along by a dark horse.

The talking turkey from Queer Street
In double Dutch conversation
Squashed the eggs into one basket.

Hatches were battened down
As in the offing ships passed in the night
Taking a hostage to fortune for the high and dry.

A long in the tooth wolf in sheep's clothing
Came under the cosh
To make the grade or fall on a sword.

In speaking of the devil
Skeletons from the closet were released
Showing true colors warts and all.

The axe long since ground down to the handle
Turns over new leaf after new leaf
Intentionally prying open Pandora's Box.

As sure as eggs is eggs
The name in the mud
Mum's the word.

# MAIGUILT

Maiguilt is full of charm,
smiling and offering her arm.
Come walk with me she will say,
on this another guilty day.
Have just one more cigarette,
make you feel better she will bet.
Pour yourself another whisky,
forget that for your liver it is risky.

Maiguilt is always at my side,
ready to cuddle arms open wide.
She says that given time,
they'll forget my guilty crime.
Maiguilt is always at my side,
my guilty secrets helping hide.
To get her to go away,
confession is the only way.

So Maiguilt from this day on,
I confess that I was wrong.
Today the twenty second of September,
from this day on I will remember.
That it is I who am to blame
no more hiding from the shame.
In everything the truth and not,
I take the blame for the lot.

# MERMAID SONG

When a fish is once caught
and gets away,
a valuable lesson is imprinted.
Making it impossible
for an attempted imprisonment twice.
For the fisher,
short term emotional satisfaction a temporary gift,
greater significance lies in the loss.

Swathed in velvet silk moonlight
the mermaid swam freely away,
sea salt stinging the wound
to cleanse and repair.
Her song drifting
in silver shards,
mingling wholly
with brine and foam.

Tapping rhythm with tail
a cry to those who hear
●●● ●_ ●●●_ ●

_ _ _●__

●●● ___ ●●_ ●_●●
Echoes longing for ingress
the mermaid sings
her sad oceans song.

# ...OF ACTIONS...

Gaze into the crying ball
Stumble in the mist
Falling and standing
Never staying down

Wave a burning sage stick
Strike it through the air
Clear that false impression
Lingering in the air

Call upon the powers
North in earthly green
South and fiery red
East wind yellow
West a watery blue

Collect fallen branches
Draw a symbolic sword
Let wind blow in the chimes
Fill a glass with water
Symbol divine in center

Count environmental sounds
Clear the space
Get thee gone
Turn the sound off and affirm

Quiet the mind
Notice the world
Visualize shape
See objects
Examine each individual piece

Use the present
Speak in positive tongue
Specify what not how
No ifs buts or maybe's

In the belief of action
Observe the virtues
Have courage
Tell the truth
Be honorable
Practice troth
Show self-discipline
Be hospitable
Industrious in worth
Accept responsibility
Be steadfast

For the sake of honor
Don't take an oath advised by another
If the persuasion speaks in tongues
Don't accept the language you don't understand.

# PARALLEL MORPHEMES OF POETRY

From the workshop comes the tapping sound
of poetry being born.
Fictitious and documentary
finding a first second and third way to phrase;
the threatening flirtation of the sky,
solemn and askew angles of life
shinning the light of vocabulary into every corner.
Oft an involuntary extinguisher,
extinguishing the:
Unproductive and poor
Abstracted and fantastical.
Questioning:
Exotic sounds in variation of format
How to define a thunderstorm
Categorical statements.
Abandonment of:
Closed formatting
Diminishing rhyme
Closed form
Stanza
Free form
Partial and rich rhymes
Exotic form
Metering four beats to a line
Any old shape and silly form,
to end stop or not that is the question.
Where to place:
Colons and semicolons
Full stops and commas
Capitalizations
To capitalize a list or not
the next line
any line
This line…
How the verses appear on the page,
how well they read out-loud.

And importantly does the poem
hold up to:
X-ray
Scrutiny
Disassembling
And whatever scholars call,
ending a poem with the title
Parallel Morphemes of Poetry.

# PAREIDOLIA

There is a face on the moon,
giving furtive glances.
A horse in the sky,
riding the storm.
On a rock a butterfly,
sitting motionless.

A tad fascinating,
but not obsessive.
I'm slightly uncontrollable,
can be rather compulsive.
It's a little chaotic,
often without disorder.

There is a man in the bark,
growing a lichen beard.
A deep eyed woman,
smiling on a stone.
On the pavement a bird,
flying nowhere.

Going around in circles,
making straight lines.
I'm often curious,
erring on the side of whimsical.
It's abstract in character,
concrete in the visual.

# TOODLE-OO

In my nest there's a Cuckoo
Causing a hullabaloo
I'm fed up with its pooh
Gonna say so-long-toodle-oo
To that tu-wit-tu-woo.

Gonna learn verbal kung-fu
With the toe of my shoe
I'll kick it up the wazoo
It's gonna meet its waterloo
With no paddle for the canoe.

Gonna wash out with shampoo
Get a new hairdo
Elbow out that cuckoo
With a quick buckaroo
Sneeze it out a-a-at-choo.

# FLAGITIOUS'S VIBRATOR.

Shut tight you potty mouth,
Keep your comments in your loo.
Can't you see we're pissed off,
With your mouth filled with pooh.
We hope you and your vibrator
Run out of batteries soon,
Ending your tales of thrusters
And how it makes you swoon.
Your talk about the real deal
Is just as fanciful and bad,
In all the places you've copped a feel
And the best screw you've ever had.
After coming into ear shot
We watch men scurry away,
If your vibrators the best you've got,
Good luck is probably what they say.
We're bored with tales from your orifices
And what's been put inside you,
Your endless talk about devices
That brings great pleasure to you.
One day we might get a shock
One day it might be true,
When you say you've had some cock
And what it did to you.

# LOVERS OF WORDS

```
                    P
THE LANGUAGE LOVERS
                    A         C
                    Y         R
                              AFTER DARK
                              B
                              B
                              L
                              E


          L
LINKED BY EACH
          T
          T
          E         D
          FORMING WORDS
                    W
                    AND ACROSS


                    T
UNITED AND CLOSE
                    G
                    E
                    T
                    H
                    E
                    SHARING TRIPLE LETTER
                    C
                    O
                    R
                    E
                    S
```

# OBVERSE INTRANSITIVE VERB.

Hold out your arms, give a fond caress,
Count the pitfalls as a blessing;
Love is the greatest weapon to possess.

Love the verb, often elusive and spurious,
A stone on which to be stepping;
Hold out your arms, give a fond caress.

A game of checking the obverse,
Of a precious coin that's flipping;
Love is the greatest weapon to possess.

Into puberty sometimes to transgress,
Within the world of expert wooing;
Hold out your arms, give a fond caress.

It's not a question of counting success,
In signs and signals most confusing;
Love is the greatest weapon to possess.

That transitive verb most happy and depressing,
Demonstrated as much in doing as saying.
Hold out your arms, give a fond caress,
Love is the greatest weapon to possess.

# SITTING PRECARIOUSLY

Sitting precariously, on the in-between fence,
Observing life's tide, coming in high going out low;
Wishing in the moonlight for clairvoyance.

There's been a test, of will and patience,
All lined up, yesterday's heroes, friend and foe;
Sitting precariously, on the in-between fence.

The one most disturbing, in the past tense,
Is the one mumbling, stay, no go on, go on;
Wishing in the moonlight for clairvoyance.

For an interlude, in the deafening silence,
Just once more to have a chattering rainbow;
Sitting precariously, on the in-between fence.

Waiting for a break, a lift in the suspense,
As ever and always, in the quiet ditto, ditto;
Wishing in the moonlight for clairvoyance.

And you may say, in this first instance,
Jump down, don't be the lonely fellow;
Sitting precariously, on the in-between fence,
Wishing in the moonlight for clairvoyance.

# BUMCAM

The topic is endoscopy
from the other end,
the patient lay quite comfortable
as the camera did ascend.
The operator of the looking device she said
"There's no feeling up there you know."
The patients intestines they apparently
had a healthy red and pink glow.
Interesting as it was, but definitely not fun,
laughter can't be hidden when my sister calls it,
The Camera Up The Bum.

# DEAR FACEBOOK

Re your sponsored links,
thanks for advising me that I'm knocking on a bit;
It's best to plan my own funeral now,
That I should be making plans for age related illnesses,
For the Mum exposing her anti-wrinkle trick,
That I am needed to volunteer for studies into cardiovascular research,
Informing me about Helen Mirren's shocking wrinkle erasing secret,
For showing me drape-dresses for the older woman,
And underwear that supports and flatters the older figure.

Yes, I am fifty nearly sixty every next birthday,
But really, I do not need reminding that:
Funerals are expensive,
Wrinkles need to be stamped out,
My heart maybe heading towards giving up
whilst bits of my body are heading down.
I'm donating me to medical science
so no funeral plans, thanks all the same.
I'm not bothered about wrinkles, kinks, sags, lumps and bumps.
Yes I sometimes quarrel with my underwear
but no more than I did at 21.
On the bright side you haven't yet
sponsored link trolled me about bladder control.
Maybe you believe I have enough age related things
to worry about buying for now.

Please inform that information gathering troll,
just because I was fifty something last birthday:
I do not intend to hide my lumps and bumps,
or go on holidays designed for extra peace and quiet.
I intend to be free, sagging and naughty right up to the end.

# FOUR VERSES OF MARRIAGE

1
They were too young
Didn't know any different
Families applied pressure
Common in its time.
The Pregnant Girl and the Bass Player
Did what was expected.
When the baby arrived
He disappeared off the scene
She felt great relief
The cause on the Decree Absolute
Dissertation.

2
Stumpy was the older man
A well respected criminal
The getaway driver of the gang
He had committed crimes and done his time
Not the sharpest tool in the shed
Doing the only thing he knew how.
She was the deliverer of goods
No questions asked
A pretty young thing
Who had earned respect by not sleeping around
Being tight lipped and trustworthy.
They worked well together for a time
Until progress took its toll.
Stumpy took to
Being on first names terms with a bookie
Watching daytime TV
Leaving dishes in the sink
Resenting her more and more.
She got herself an education
Turned into a Rita of her time
Changed beyond recognition
Started legitimate employment.

136

Stumpy resented her new persona
How squeaky clean she had become
He felt awkward and left behind.
She started to dislike the old man
How he looked and smelt
The resentment in his eyes.
The cause on the Decree Absolute
Irretrievable Breakdown.

3
He whose name she doesn't speak
A knight in shining armour at first
Master of the psychological arts
A manipulating wolf in sheep's clothing
On the outside he encouraged her
Inside he wore her down.
She slowly submitted to domination
It didn't happen overnight
Hiding bruises
Apologizing for bad behavior
Dressing more appropriately
Submitting to doing as she was told.
The girl who had earned respect
One day returned from out of the blue
Came close to inserting a building brick
Deep inside his nasty head.
The cause on the Decree Absolute
Unreasonable Behaviour.

4
Howdy was the true one
Hard working Mr Right
With a proper job with prospects
Ambitions for the future
A life history similar to hers.
With joint dreams being fulfilled

Money and prospects came rolling in
With supportive care and respect
Together they moved on up
Planned a happily ever after ending.
Until the cause on the death certificate
Pancoast Tumour.

# MR. WOLF

Whatever his title might be
He's at my heels again
After dinner mints in pocket
To clear his rasping throat
Suited up and booted

Trousers crisply pressed
He is a handsome devil
Exquisitely he is dressed

Tip toeing quietly behind me
In step behind with every pace
Must resist the urge to make him
Exclaim the time is one o'clock

Must not look him in the eyes
Remain steadfast face the front

Whenever he is behind me
Out there in my shadow
Let me please be strong enough
For turning will make me dinner.

# PAVLOV'S BEAST

Something hideous reared its ugly head, rolled around a thick strong neck.

One snap at a time it's prickly spine uncurled, until the beast raised high on its haunches, gave a satisfactory moan of accomplishment.

The beast stands firm, unfolded and freely occupying space with pain educing determination, furious anger ooze from bitter red eyes.

Fingers flexed, curled making a fist, flexed and curled, flexed, curled, flexed; knuckles cracked breaking morbid silence.

A gnarled finger with a long sharp yellow nail at the tip, thrusts forward, points, stabs the air.

With rasping foul breath, in a contaminating black fume spurious mockery spews out stigmatizing with fervor.

It smiles at the achievement, grins at the accomplishment of its purpose.

Animated and herculean in the task, stagnant still waters with little effort stirred to life.

The legacy on the beasts dying breath, kept alive by the curse.

Purgatory and all its damnations are my gift to you, when the bell rings;

You and Your Children will feel the acrid warmth of my breath, feel the pain of my legacy and I will forever be resurrected and set free to burden you with condemnation and shame.

I will not allow the cycle to be broken, I will be resurrected;

Unlocked

Released

Unleashed

Keeping you in your place through the power of guilt and pain.

You will become the beast in my place, when I ring the bell you will jump as high as I told you to.

This is my legacy, your inheritance a conditioned reflex, its stimuli reaching far from beyond the grave.

Long after death intervenes, Pavlov's beast lives on.

# ERROR ME THIS???

Clogged up to hell and back
On the verge of breaking down
Missing links and virtual errors
Plagued by a clanking sound
Undone some reconnected some more
To make more space deleted
E-Books read and photographs saved
Round the system removing I go

Even the home-screen links binned
Removed till desktop clean
Rampaging error messages.

Wait data loading
No it's not
Oh why are you still seen?
Right where did I put that stick?

# DING DING BENDY BUS

Jump on the go straight bendy bus
Sit on a worn out seat of hundreds before
Try to look out the window
But it's all steamed up
Oh no no no no no
No no don't turn right

Oh no no no no no
No no please go left
Wrong number
Wrong way
Wrong destination
Oh no no no no no
Oh no not lost again

Ding ding ding ding ding
Driver stop now please
Ding ding ding ding ding
Driver stop for me

Step off onto a worn out street
Where hundreds of feet have gone before
Where walkers dance the walkers dance
Slow slow excuse me please
Slow slow quick quick slow

Some going up
Some staying where they are
Some coming down
Some crossing to the other side
Slow slow quick quick slow

Some run to the keep left island
Keeping right depending on side
Passenger off the wrong bendy bus
Standing still trying to decide
To go left and be right
Go right and be left
On the other side.

# ELEPHANT IN THE ROOM

On the rampage there is an Elephant in the room.
Indiscriminately stomping around;
huge body mass knocking over all it can,
trampling and squashing emotions,
it lifts them with its ivory protuberances, shakes them loose,
picks them up again, chucks them around, revives them and repeats.
With beady eyes as it follows every move it threatens destruction.
Its loud call reverberates around the space,
shattering glass and penetrating the walls.
The dust it has caused remains unsettled and weighs heavy,
makes breathing and seeing difficult.
Every move the Elephant makes
shifts tectonic plates causing cracks to appear,
foundations rock as the ground opens up and swallows before spewing out again.
The circus of life continues,
the Elephant in the room the main attraction.
It sways from side to side
as it contemplates its next assault with more rocking,
withdrawing, attacking, destroying...
The Elephant is unchained and has escaped from the room
it is running down the street,
it is out there now and has already caused mass destruction.

# AGAIN...

Again...
> The devil's own handsome rookie
> Took a real good look at me
> He asked me for my number
> I gave it coz I'm dumber.

Again...
> I really should know better
> Though behind my ears still wetter
> Never too old for romantic stuff
> Kicking up heels and playing rough.

Again...
> Lying got right to me
> Waded through it to the knee
> Till I walked in another direction
> Breaking all connection.

Again...
> Next time I'll look much closer
> And see beyond the poser.

# DRIFTWOOD

What fate
Brought you close to me.
I wonder at
Your journey.
Who was it that
Discarded you?
What man's machine?
Cut down
Your prime.
You have become
Seas burden.
For only she
Could carry your
Huge mass.
Was it a boat?
Or at least twenty men
That gave you
To her.
Becoming my temporary
Resting place.
I'm sure
Was never your plan.
As I sit
On your green slimy coverage.
Watching her turn
Head in.
If today
She is high
Tomorrow
You'll be gone.
I might stand
Where once was you.
Starring out
Into many miles.
What was it?
What events?

Turned rooted
Blowing in breeze.
To turning
Under wave.
Time for me
To leave.
She is close now
Sand is getting wet.
I envy you
No decisions to make.
Kept new
By the freedom
Of the seas choice.

# EXTRACT FROM THE POETS STATEMENT:

I admit that I was there in Kent, honestly it's just coincidental,
the ropes, whips, handcuffs and chains, forensics will find them coincidental.
Yes, of course you will find my DNA, on glasses and stools in the Cellar Bar,
I confess to being there at the time in question, but harm her without permission goes too far.
She's told me all about Ms Poppet Malone, no I've never met her we only chat online,
where we exchange cooking and make-up tips from time to time.
It really is more likely that she would murder me,
for my crimes against poetry.
I said that heavy blue eye shadow gave out the wrong signals, really was just a matter of time,
before she attracted the attention of some filthy obsessive swine.
Of course I went to admire at her at a distance, I went to kent,
I had a good look and then gave her up for lent.
Me and Flame let's be honest, it was just never meant to be,
but harm her, never, not a single hair on her pretty head, it wasn't me.
Now I know how this works, seen detectives on a television show,
so bang me up, charge me, punish me or let me go.

# IT MIGHT BE TRUE

Conventional relationships and me
                              don't mix well…
Too much…
               downtrodden uncommon ground
fast flowing water gone under the bridge.
Conspicuous absences…
never discussed.

Too many multiplications x x x
ending in subtraction -.

Still I'm a sucker for creative intelligence
that's what draws me in.
Not the way one looks
or what is said
it's a common view
occasionally tugs this thread.
I get drawn in……….pulled towards
frequently when resistance proves pointless
With reverberating recoil…
                              .the thread snaps.

You undeniably confuse me.
With you the thread of connection
Tightens
as we pull together
Slackens
hanging between we two
always there.

You absolutely bewilder me.
I put myself in your hands
your tactics draw me in
make me a part of the scheme.
You…
        select and deduce…
                        consort and associate…
                                        draw and derive…
        with your magnetism…

I become your accessory
You become my accomplice

As is now the routine
the thread slackens
as we shy away
shrink back
step aside
withdraw in unflinching retraction.

There is grandiosity in all this
not sure if it's yours or mine
projection is in there somewhere.
Like all machines
Sometimes
It
Breaks
Down
But the
Components
Are still
There.

# TAKING THE BISCUIT FOR AN IDIOM SWIM

Wearing an old hat
I carried water to the river,
Sat on a bridge over troubled water
Pausing only to read the writing on the wall;
As much water flowed under the bridge
I tentatively dipped my toes in the water,
And observed the baby and the bathwater
Float away to cloud cuckoo land.

The horse that brought me to where
Still waters run deep,
Kept its head above water
And did not drink a drop;
As is the rule of thumb
The horse continued to tread water,
And a fish came out of the water
Searching for a bed of roses.

To add insult to injury
Old Man Codswallop,
Caught between the devil and the deep blue sea
Poured oil on the troubled waters;
Made of sterner stuff
The sitting pretty ducks,
Let the muddied water
Roll off their backs.

# THE CARETAKERS CUPBOARD

From way up there on moral high ground,
Inside the desolate inner sanctum of the mind,
Where lost dragon's teeth leave empty holes
And trees are cut down from their roots;
From out of the caretaker's cupboard they come,
Where hot sweet tea is cheap and sugar cubes poisonous,
They heckle and spit out the words,
"You can't go back to masks and curtains, not anymore."

The duty of the performer at the trial,
Is to bail out for appearance at a later date,
To slip and slide through the quagmire
And jump from floating leaves too paper boats;
Without a paddle,
Attempt blind steps backwards,
Blindfolded movements forwards,
As the slimy sticky mixture sticks firm.

Way up there on dubiously principled high ground,
The rights and wrongs in behaviour,
Rattle around in a malleable tin
Controlled by outside forces and influences;
Bitter pills regurgitated,
Pour into a bucket of slop and vulgarity,
That caretakers store in their evidence cupboard,
For use when the trail resumes.

# TUESDAY OVER 14'S DISCO

I put on my platform shoes
and a pair of Oxford Bags;
tuck a book of matches down one sock
and in the other one 10 Sovereign fags.

My teardrop collar and turn back cuffs
are really still very damp;
Mam warns – you'll get a cold
and later arthritis and cramp.

As I'm heading out the door
Dad sneaks me an extra ten pence;
and says – go before your Mother
washes that war paint off your face.

We meet at the post box on the corner,
Me, my best friends Sherfield and little Yvonne;
share a flagon of Woodpecker cider
and agree liking Donny Osmond is wrong.

When we get to the Top Rank
the two Tonys are on the door;
we hand them our complimentary tickets
and head straight onto the dance floor.

We met some boys from Mumbles
who taught us a new skinhead dance;
the one I fancied was really posh
he'd been on holiday to France.

The posh boy gave Sherfield a love bite,
a big purple one almost on her chin;
when we get to her house I'm glad it wasn't me,
coz she's scared when she goes in.

# TERATOLOGY NIGHTMARE

Monitoring every shift in air pressure;
Compulsively,
Excessively,
Territorially,
In closed guarded secrecy.
Affected responsibility, seeps through veins;
Animated by glorified sensationalism.
Fashioned in lunacy and dementia, obstinately old;
Classical manifestations of Sunday's self-righteous,
Creep from pillars of salt to outposts.
Fuelled by the exploitative apoplectic rage;
Of predecessors whom are idolised and worshiped.

Peeling off corridors into darkened spaces;
Toothlessly grinning as pleasant as tooth loss itself,
To lurk behind wooden barriers and peepholes.
Fastidious methodologies of dross ridden hypocrisy;
Form the chorus of the hymn of destruction of youth,
The wag-on-the-wall keeps time in the past.
Those who would throw themselves under horses;
Turn uncomfortably from shallow graves,
As they move through the ark of the circle unnoticed.
Keeping themselves non participatory safe;
Just outside of the boundaries, looking in on the,
Seriocomic nature of a teratology nightmare.

# MADNESS FOR NUMEROUS SECONDS

When the memory beckons,
Calls forth sorrow from its sojourn;
There's madness for numerous seconds.

Suddenly breaking silence comments,
Runs boldly across a patterned lawn;
When the memory beckons.

With the breaking of the seals.
Releasing the lost and forlorn;
There's madness for numerous seconds.

Varied in form and manifestations,
History repeated once again reborn;
When the memory beckons.

With light illuminating transgressions,
Through curtains tattered and torn;
There's madness for numerous seconds.

Caught in a net of committed sins,
Of promises broken and easily sworn.
When the memory beckons,
There's madness for numerous seconds.

# MENTAL HEALTH VILLANELLE

How does one begin to frankly say?
Help, I'm definitely broken;
I've lost the plot along the way.

And it continues on from yesterday,
This persistent growing mutagen;
How does one begin to frankly say?

That days are tones of black and grey,
Within this persistent given;
I've lost the plot along the way.

And when tomorrow becomes a today,
I will still be very broken;
How does one begin to frankly say?

Help me, I don't want to play,
Please read the signs unspoken;
I've lost the plot along the way.

Whatever, and come what may,
The mental health monsters awoken.
How does one begin to say?
I've lost the plot along the way.

# NOT A VILLANELLE

So I waste time writing nonsense
In the form of short verse,
And for just a few minutes
I can alleviate the thinking curse,
Of my head being in pieces
And how to stop it getting worse.

By thinking about couplets
And how many in the rhyme,
Is as good a way as any
For wasting precious time,
Whilst trying to discover
What's going on in this head of mine?

When I'm on a poetry roll
Time passes in a blink,
And best of all
I don't stop to think,
That outside of my poetry box
How life is such a stink.

# MIDWAY TRYING VILLANELLE

Keep on trying patiently to see it through,
Tomorrow will be another keep trying day;
Keep a hold of this is what I came here to do.

Past offensive hurts, to try and undo,
From the difficult end goal not to stray;
Keep on trying patiently to see it through.

And scrape off yesteryears heavy mildew,
Pay close attention to what they need to say;
Keep a hold of this is what I came here to do.

It's been way too long since we withdrew,
Time to finally end condemning hearsay;
Keep on trying patiently to see it through.

Stains of bygones heavily they accrue,
Overdue for their air dirty laundry day;
Keep a hold of this is what I came here to do.

It's time to move from under this cloud so blue,
Put aside the words we can't take back, unsay.
Keep on trying patiently to see it through,
Keep a hold of this is what I came here to do.

# EARLY FTD VILLANELLE

Becoming a walking talking villanelle,
Front Temporal Dementia could be taking over;
Complete with incompetence of how to spell.

Process of having a tale to tell,
Playing Russian roulette with vocabulary revolver;
Becoming a walking talking villanelle.

Memory may completely leave nutshell,
Dwindle itself away in misbehavior;
Complete with incompetence of how to spell.

Thoughts are becoming a Scarlet Pimpernel,
If a dog they'd be called Rover;
Becoming a walking talking villanelle.

In the future words could go to hell,
Along with ability for technical maneuvers;
Complete with incompetence of how to spell.

It's time to cram in while still able,
Before ability gets any further lower.
Becoming a walking talking villanelle,
Complete with incompetence of how to spell.

# I AM WAITING

(Villanelle Part 1)
For sorry but it is no with regret,
On another waiting day;
I continue to smoke another cigarette.

And wait to see if criteria is met,
Or if the usual answer comes, no way;
For sorry but it is no with regret.

The balls been rolled, the scene been set,
On another wait and see day;
For sorry but it is no with regret.

Waiting to learn if help I'll get,
Could be yes, might also be nay;
I continue to smoke another cigarette.

How long I've waited, I forget,
For whatever, come what may;
For sorry but it is no with regret.

The actions have been made, scene been set,
On this another wait and see day.
For sorry but it is no with regret,
I continue to smoke another cigarette.

# I AM WAITING

(Villanelle Part 2)
As day will meander into night,
With the coming of the end of a closing day;
I feel like a diminishing light.

My head is broken, it's not right,
They make it worse when nothing they say;
As day will meander into night.

Where's she gone? Her who shinned so bright,
Only one description left today;
I feel like a diminishing light.

Caught between flight and fight,
Hoping help is on its way;
As day will meander into night.

My head is broken, I have no sight;
I have lost the path along the way;
I feel like a diminishing light.

Left to wait for those on height,
To listen to the word's I say.
My head is broken, I have no sight,
I feel like a diminishing light.

# I AM WAITING

(Villanelle Part 3)
Slowly the poison drips and fills,
This heavy weight and wait it tires;
Wasting time, it kills and kills.

In your system, of wait until,
You decide what my life requires;
Slowly the poison drips and fills.

It has a label bearing no frills,
She doesn't know what she desires;
Wasting time, it kills and kills.

But to wait and wait to climb more hills,
Until the day that she retires;
Slowly the poison drips and fills.

No longer to shout in shrills,
Give up trying to spark the fires;
Wasting time, it kills and kills.

In poems dumped all lost ills,
As missing dates like the heart expires.
Slowly the poison drips and fills.
Wasting time, it kills and kills.

# I AM WAITING

(Villanelle Part 4)
Waiting for tears that never swell,
No crying is so damned unfair;
So I wrote another villanelle.

With a voice akin to a faint little bell,
All been tried, including prayer;
While waiting for tears that never swell.

Help there maybe, who can tell,
Waiting under a cloud of despair;
I go on and write another villanelle.

Perhaps I need something surgical,
Or developed a condition even more unfair;
Than waiting for tears that never swell.

When everything seems so diabolical,
Shredded more with every no coming tear;
I get on with another villanelle.

Waiting for the positive, not whimsical,
Waiting for more time to tell.
Waiting for tears that don't swell.
All that's left is another villanelle.

# AROUND ANOTHER BEND

The road keeps curving and changing shape,
There is no clear sight of the road ahead,
Around every bend;
Lies more confusion and questions.
All answers pose a question and a could be,
Maybe next week, perhaps the week after,
Possibly the month after that;
Conceivably sometime,
But never in the here and now
Of today or tomorrow.

# UNTITLED PERPETUUM

The silken she wolf is at the door,
In she meanders with stealth and beauty;
In coming to build further upon rapport.

Between the odd job and domestic chore,
Completed with skill and professionality;
The silken she wolf is at the door.

Her intentions come with no underscore,
It's all read between the lines metaphysically;
In coming to build further upon rapport.

The half-light of lightning and thunder's roar,
With trepidation and much complexity;
The silken she wolf is at the door.

Wearing a finely woven masculine roquelaure,
Inducing the urge to covet incessantly;
In coming to build further upon rapport.

There is difficulty in subtle equilibrium to restore,
When there are smiles nervous and invitingly.
The silken she wolf is at the door,
In coming to build further upon rapport.

# TWO SHE'S

Tripping in, she wears slippers,
Strolling in, she wears sandals;
Both tread carefully over skeletons,
In an effort to build bridges
Across aging scars and ridges.

She wants to appear omnifarious,
Shy and alluringly curious;
About delights of being promiscuous,
She tries to stay ambiguous,
Wishing to avoid anything tempestuous.

She is more transpicuous,
With a dress code that says amorphous;
There's no mistaking her earnestness,
Nothing about her is conspicuous,
Her sexuality is out and obvious.

Neither wants to be presumptuous,
Approaching with an air of cautiousness;
Whilst trying to each keep their focus,
Before crossing the boundaries of friendship,
To enter the same sex world of relationships.

# DAWN CHORUS

In near rhythm, in almost perfect time,
Focusing on each other's moves before they came,
They were close to the end, so close they could smell it,
The aroma of attraction hanging heavy between them.

When the anticipation in the waiting, promises more than sex,
What does it matter how long the climax is in coming.
Trying not to be amber gamblers, each awaits the green light,
The signal that says yes go, I am, and we are ready.

With many trophies under their belts, each has experience,
In dancing to the song of lust, of wanting and waiting,
For the signal to change from maybe to yes.

In their private fantasies, each imagines the grabbing of hands,
That movement into the starting position;
To the feel of breast against breast, both smelling so good,
Until finally comes the exhilaration of sharing the same bed.

In wanting more, much more than friendship,
They both new their moves weren't tidy, not neat but awkward;
Each fed up of being alone and knowing,
If doesn't happen soon the opportunity may pass.

Greeting each other enthusiastically with flirtatious smiles,
With the almost unbearable sensation of hands that almost touch;
Tense bodies trying not to occupy each other's spaces,
Each wanting more, much more, but afraid to say.

Until it came, a simultaneous release of trust,
Both leaning forward at the same time, warm lips engaging a kiss;
Leading to waking each new day into a dawn chorus of,
Knowing this is what they both want.

# GETTING AHEAD OF MYSELF

Ahead of the day beginning,
When a soft pillow still envelops your mind;
While your inhibitions are still free
Walking barefoot through a bluebell woods,
I will be alongside you.

When the alarm rings time to wake,
Bringing you into the land of consciousness:
And you wipe the slumber from your eyes
Considering getting a start to your day,
I will put a mug of coffee in your hands.

Once you've showered away the night,
And dressed for another day at work;
Turned your phone on in preparation
And placed your work things by the door,
I will put breakfast on your plate.

When your working day is done,
And you get yourself a cold beer;
Then fall into your favorite comfy chair
Offloading the days woes and pleasures,
I will listen and understand.

At the end of the day,
When you lay in bed tired and worn out,
Speaking of relief that tomorrows Friday
And that the weekend will be ours,
I will rub your shoulders till you sleep.

As I enter the land of consciousness,
Realizing your lying next to me was a dream;
And I have a cup of coffee alone
Whilst you're out there preparing for your day,
I will prepare to tell you, today I will say it, I love you.

# HESITERERUMTATION

Um...err – ah... um er
Think about hesitation for five she said,
Er – arrrr – um...oh – arg
Oh no my brain is empty.

Calm down, er-um
No, I can't calm down
I've already wasted two and a half minutes
Cough – arrr – clear the throat.
Long silent pauses are in my head
Nowt, zilch, nothing, ooh arr err um

Um – er – oh dear
I've hesitated way too long
And now times
Almost up

Um....err – ah...um er
Oh well oh dear
Oh I give in
Hesitations won.

# TO TRULY DEFEAT AN ENEMY

To truly defeat an enemy, you must know them better than yourself.

There are those who do fighting and those who do dying, whilst God doesn't even get his feet wet

Keep all armour in good order, it may be heavy but in times of battle you will need your protection, to guard you well.

When the question is, do you feel better or worse and the answer is neither, it is time to move on.

Don't fear the making of the first move.

Hopeless is the stuff of legends, hopeless is what they write songs about. When charms and amulets don't work, there is always your friend stealth and war.

Finding someone who speaks your language requires a wandering tongue, the completion of a search may also depend on silence.

To stem bleeding, a wound must be tightly bound and cleansed.

Not accepting food from strangers is foolish, but better to die poisoned with a full belly, than to die empty and hungry.

What cruel devises does fate hold in store?

How many more Demons disguised as Angels are there left to encounter and fight.

Ride out the storm, seek shelter if you can.

Don't let blue skies give false security, always be prepared for heavy rain and thunder bolts with lighting.

Ignore the shrill screams, but heed the sound of pain, learn well and keep the mask up.

# VASO ATTACK

After last night's news,
There will now be the waiting for the physical reaction.
No longer able to scream and cry in pain,
The brain will disconnect.
Without warning,
Shut down.
The scars from the last one,
Still visible on the face.
Grief anger and sadness,
Now expressed this way.
Knowing what the response should be,
Not reacting as others do.
Persons for whom no love is lost,
Have abruptly left the mortal plain.
Now the waiting in caution,
To awaken bruised and bleeding.
Things need avoiding,
Until after it has been.
Giving little signal or warning,
Coming out of the blue.
Not totally unexpected,
Timing will be unknown.
Each one leaves behind,
Physical scars and wounds.
Injuries to the heart,
Manifest as scars on the face.
Each one a physical reminder,
Of heartaches of the past.

# ABSENCE TOO LONG FREQUENCIES

Today I wear my funeral attire
Nobody died.
It's just a black fashion day.
To brighten
Or not
With a silk patterned red and yellow scarf.
Doesn't feel right,
So I dig out the black and grey one.
Looking in the mirror
I see funerals past.
The husband, the family, the friends.
All stare back in the reflection
Reminding me of black fragility.
When I go
I want no absence of light.
Long frequencies only will be allowed.
No secondary and tertiary
Primaries only
For the optical mix.
In my mind
I observe how the colours blend.
Reds and yellows
Optically mixing.
Creating a warm orange glow.
Blues and reds
Give an ecclesiastical air.
Today is now
A bright colours day.
With complimentary
Trousers and jumper.
Opposites on the colour wheel.
The absence of light
Hangs back in the wardrobe.

# THE PROSPECT OF SIGNIFICANT OTHER

Amongst the disagreeable projections
Omitting from royalty and commanders alike,
She is fleet of movement
With sweet and firm fluency;
In one lithe and steadfast bound
She scales a brick wall,
Careful to avoid the meeting of anyone,
Entering only by the backdoor,
Into a sanctuary that's not a retreat,
But a fleeting temporary refuge from turmoil.
The cause and effect one and the same,
The pros and the cons both on either side
Bring about bewilderment and perplexity,
As the scales of probability
Tip this way and that with equal ferocity;
Never settling on an equilibrium.

The conversation is fraught with stalling gestures,
Words become improper and misunderstood,
As Arms fold tightly across beautiful breasts,
When there is dryness of mouth and licking of lips
Conversation is neither possible nor enough,
As eyes are difficult to pin to one place;
Amidst growls of dissatisfaction
And the biting of nails,
Comes the furtive glancing at a clock
That never indicates the right time.
Resorting to quips and puns
Meant to cover up uncertainty,
Only further succeed to humiliate and fluster
As they expose hidden hopes and dreams.

The other woman
Unsure of her significance,
Waits with patience and trepidation
As her shrouded history is revealed;

173

Almost instantaneously she is exposed,
Raw and smarting she stutters
Mispronouncing words over and over again,
As each question is answered with a question,
And doubt is piled upon certainty,
Comes the tight shoulders
And rapid blinking and breaths.
Reactive emotions take control
Making logical decision impossible,
Suffering from nothing to give;
The sensation of dryness
Overwhelms and characterizes
Every means to an end taken.

Tensions that cut like ice
And soothe like the summer sun,
Give courage to take the force of the blow,
Shoulders back and chest out
With hips firmly in place;
Exhibiting much needed protection,
The liability has been accepted.
The banner of test and confirmation
Has been run up the flagpole,
Rippling in the slightness of breeze;
As history threatens to repeat itself
With shuddering rendition,
The verb that is never spoken clearly
Is once more skirted over,
Only mentioned as an abstract prospect.
The basic principles of a strategy
Fall to the wayside,
As the doing word entices and consumes,
Fears of keeping silence and missed opportunities;
Gives way to chance taking
And the prospect of a significant other,
With a sharp intake and release of breath
Reaches realization.

# TWITCHERS

Here comes the Moon
All shine and action,
In her white metal steed
The writing on the side
Gives her away,
It proclaims
I am here.
She's going to call in,
Maybe, definitely,
Curtain twitchers
Cop an eyeful
Phones at the ready,
Oo you'll never guess
She's having her way over there,
It's against the rules
And I haven't been fucked
Since oh! About 1972.

Well listen here,
You dried up
Bored miserable old fuck,
Get yourself a wank
Or if you dare
Get the real thing.
Stop twitching
For the wrong reasons,
Imagining intertwined legs
And wondering
How do two women do it?
Are they doing it now?
Which one is the man?
Putting the kettle on
In between twitching
Doing what you always do
Have a cup of tea
And imagine in loneliness
Two women fucking.

# DRY STORM

With an overwhelming need to lay on the divan,
Desiring much more than, this was my day intercourse;
In dealing with the complexities of being woman to woman.

So many difficulties and pitfalls surrounding the current location,
Numerous turning up of old stones from inside a glass house;
With an overwhelming desire to lay on the divan.

Restrictive dryness that has come from being an older woman,
Constricting and painful where there should be an exudence of juice;
In dealing with the complexities of being woman to woman.

Amongst dealing with fears that this gift horse is a Trojan,
The doing word has become more obtuse;
With an overwhelming desire to lay on the divan.

Actions are clouded, no words accurate and spick and span,
When conveying emotions and putting them to good use;
In dealing with the complexities of being woman to woman.

The arrangement of parts of the anatomy clouds the ethos,
When being defined by gender and history, not by the person;
With an overwhelming desire to lay on the divan,
In dealing with the complexities of being woman to woman.

# LAST CHANCE SALOON

Intoxication coming from inside
Stops me dead in my stride,
One last time I stand
With the palm of my uneasy hand,
On the door of my last chance saloon.

Bottles line shelves on the bar
With labels from near and far,
My glass is empty and I want more
And all I can do is stand at the door,
Of my last chance saloon.

Sensations beckon me come on in
As my patience is wearing thin,
For what I'm being denied
My frustration I cannot hide,
Right now! I need to open the last chance saloon door.

I turn to thoughts of getting old
And wonder why I always feel so damned cold,
Take my hand on and off the saloon door
Then put it back again and again once more,
But pain stops me dead from opening the door.

Don't know how long I'll have to stand
With pain on the other side of my hand,
Don't know when I'll be able to begin
Allowing touching and going deep within,
The door of my last chance saloon.

Doctors have prescribed pills and potions,
Filled me up with remedies and notions,
They've turned me on my back and on my side
And said best not they go inside,
The door to my last chance saloon.

There is nothing I can do but wait
To attend a looming hospital date,
But this is driving me insane
The frustration and the pain,
Inside the door to my last chance saloon.

# EXHAUSTED

Sick and tired
Of being sick and tired,
With faulty wiring
So exposed and fraying;
No matter how much insulation
Wraps around to give protection,
Fire keeps on breaking out
In the form of worry and doubt.
Inside lips there's soreness and grazes
Cutting through each fold long ways,
Dryness occupies every crevice and crack
As we reach the point of no turning back;
And begin the much repeated game
Of who is with most fault and blame?
And now comes the point of no return
Brow beaten in another lesson to learn.
We are both so sick and tired
Of being so sick and tired,
Each the same in a much a different way
With pretty much the same things to say;
In angry texts and down the phone
Go away and leave me alone,
Followed by sorry and reconciliation
Then we repeat the same condemnation.
So now we are at the point of the end
Time for mixed messages stopping to send,
Neither of us has strength for eye to eye
Exhausted from continually asking why;
The conversation it has to be clearly made
Leaving feelings of not making the grade,
We are both too many worlds and lives apart
And now deal with a once more broken heart.
As plans for the future dissipate
Like burnt out ashes in a fire grate,
With only deep wounds left to lick
And beating ourselves with a stick;

To sick and tired to regurgitate
It's ok Babe I can wait,
We both know we tried and failed
That our ship has definitely sailed.
For that there is shared responsibility
Each must face our own liability,
In saying words meaningless and obtuse
Tripping off the tongue nasty and loose;
Each entrenched in the others crime
Equally with the blame is all mine,
Now we must turn and walk a separate way
Exhausted from what we did and didn't say.

# ONLY THROUGH CLOTH

Beneath her hardened exterior
And beyond her power tools,
Past the deep pockets of her trousers
Full of old thread-less screws;
I found a silken interior
Like I'd never experienced before.

Underneath her work shirt
There was womanhood pretty, pert and firm,
And below her waist line
A smoothness carefully shaved;
None of which I truly experienced
Apart from fleetingly, and through cloth.

New underwear I'd carefully selected
Was only briefly touched and never seen,
What was it between life's nasty sheets?
That made two excited experienced women
Ashamed of what laid beneath the cloth.
It's too late now,
Our brief encounter is over,
We're done,
So I'll never truly know her;
Only what I felt through cloth.

# ...ORICAL

The hypersensitive metaphorical
In words tight but loose,
Has become concrete allegorical
Confusing and obtuse,
No potions that are topical
Have proved to have use;
None of this is logical
It's borderline self-abuse,
Too much on the biological
To turn over again and muse,
That now it's categorical
No one wins we lose.

# WHY?

Arriving at a river and
Discovering no bridges,
Not a single stepping stone
Or shallow ford to walk.
A further enquiry followed by
Just one more question
Answered with another question,
Replying with a question
As requests turn to demands
Following query after query.
The empty space between inquiries
Filled with insecurities and possibly,
Enveloped in the bondages
Of false hope and optimism.
Becoming ever-more the fugitive
Refraining from speaking any further,
For fear of something unequivocal
Tainted with tears and antagonism.
The mouth falls shut
Wishing to speak no further,
Of mechanisms that caused sorrow
During the labor of love,
There is only backing into a corner.
All that remains is to halt reactions
Concede happiness is incomprehensible,
Curtail, make less painful the cut,
Accept the bridge was imaginary
Conceded to defeat and move on.
Ending with an unanswerable question
Answered with an unanswerable question,
Why?

# ENDING IN INFLAMMATORY EPOCH

A familiar song of lust and intrigue,
It was a fairy tale of possibilities,
Hot and intense,
With much faith in future observations;
Immersion and trust,
Entwined in blind faith and happiness.

For a few short months,
It was heartwarming and birds sang,
Until appeared the other significant other,
That breaking day the telephone rang;
With a message clear – go away leave us alone,
Bringing about the mechanism for the big bang.

In blinded hope for the future,
There was so much based on trust,
And as always clear in hindsight.
Mostly a relationship fueled by lust;
Until that Tuesday afternoon phone call,
When all became broke and bust.

Out of the blue, unexpectedly,
Becoming the prisoner in loves dock,
Being found guilty by association,
An off the Richter scale shock;
In the indirect undetectable variables,
Of the now inflammatory epoch.

# AGAIN I… AND AGAIN…

I fell in love again,
Had a moment in the sun;
Felt shelter from the rain,
In you I found the one
With love to give again.

There were smiles again,
As two became one;
With all to gain,
In feeling we had won
A prize with all to gain.

So it's happened again,
With what I haven't done;
Easy comes the pain,
I've made me alone
As no doubt I will again.

# FOR K

(Thank-you for making me feel like a teenager again)

Keep me close, as lovers turned enemies are best kept that way,
And keep a place for me in your uncertain of want heart.
Run away for now to maybe return someday, and
Envelope me in the softness you're keeping hidden from view,
No-one is ever meant to truly see, well I did. I witnessed your gentleness.

After all now, all is almost said and done,
No-one pushed my buttons as
Delicately and ferociously as did you.

So now you're over there, and I am over here
Under my handmade blanket of distrust and bad mood,
Self-pitying and wondering if the right decision was made,
And in setting you free did you go backwards or did you never leave there?
Not knowing is I fear as hard as knowing if you didn't tell the truth.

# K'S DISTRACTION

No matter what says my heart,
I was simply your distraction, that I know;
Still you send my emotions off the chart.

You entered my safely constructed habitat,
Then forced me abruptly to let you go;
No matter what says my heart.

Even though it broke me to watch you depart,
I watch for your return through my window;
Still you send my emotions off the chart.

You told me that for you, I am just to smart,
Though not clever enough to see I was your sideshow;
No matter what says my heart.

And yes my love, I also played my meagre part,
Encouraged us, didn't try to take it slow;
Still you send my emotions off the chart.

For you, I wish only a bright warm glow,
Don't know if I should hide or should show;
No matter what says my heart,
Still you send my emotions off the chart.

# THE EX

It was a very short time of glee,
That was all a whimsical farce;
First you spoke of love, then the label,
I am now The Ex.

Becoming the name that preceded me,
Referred to by you only as;
The name of all the others you call,
The Ex.

Only now it is occurring to me,
As the hurt is coming to pass;
It was simply my time to wear the shawl,
That hides the identity of The Ex.

There will be no returning to me,
I've been knocked clean onto my arse;
Now I've cried and I have bawled,
I'm happy to unidentified as The Ex.

# BI THE WAY, I'M A HUMAN BEING

A product of society
Battle scared and weary,
From querying abbreviations
Applied to sexuality;
Being sometimes pink
And sometimes blue,
And a muddied combination
Of both those two.

To add to complications
In not being perceptible,
Combined with the masculine
And the matriarchal;
Amidst concerns that the two
Are not fusible,
Leaves an initialism
Wholly unrecognizable.

Having been categorized
From being Fem too disabled,
And being neither here nor there
With a tendency to being paralleled;
Broken into acronym and half words,
Being just a human being
Who is happily excited,
With a tendency to be
A coin that's double sided.

# CAUTION

(After the poem 'Warning' by Jenny Joseph)

When I am older than the old dear I am now,
I will wear a red velvet hat that emphasizes the wrinkles.
And I shall waste my money on loose companions
And drink Harvey Wall Bangers through a bendy straw.
I will lay on a park bench in a sultry pose
And give up being veggie and eat Big Macs
And cast aside my respectable age in exchange for disgrace.
I will go out in a white T-shirt with no bra in the rain
I will get a full head of beaded dreadlocks and string wraps
And learn to speak and write like Benjamin Zephaniah
And learn to rap.
The partner in my life will wear red gold and green
And will be a lapsed vegi or vegan
And we will enjoy a full English for supper every night
We will wear Parkas decorated with badges
And have hand painted peace symbols on the back.
But for today I must continue with respectability
And go the Post office to pay my bills
At least try to be eloquent and respectable
I must take home Cod and Chips and put them on a plate.
Maybe I will begin my metamorphosis tomorrow
Some would say I'm already half way there
I think the orange leggings and purple striped top
Gives me away.

# WEIRD

From the perspective of psychology
Everyone is at least fractionally weird.
I appear to regularly become weirder,
From the psychologists weird perspective
Is that good bad weird or indifferent.

How is weird measured?
Is there a profoundly weird measurement?
And who measures the weirdos
That measure weirdness?
Is there a weirdness assessment panel?

Do they have weird letters after their names?
And use unpronounceable weird words?
Whilst dressed in weird caps and gowns
Disseminating weird advice to weirdos,
And hold conferences to debate weirdness.

And teach lessons in weirdness theory
And how to be weirdly the best weirdo,
Weirdly encouraging participation
In weird and wonderful things,
Through the weirdness of social interaction.

Weirdly strange and unusually weird
Oddly enough and weird to explain,
Everything just gets weirder and weirder
Perhaps it's just me
Getting weirder in my own little weirdo way.

# THE BED WE MADE FROM IT

Prepared with fresh cotton linen,
Every day our bed was further made;
Until was the time to lay on it.

At night when at first climbing in,
Wishing to get back the scent;
Laundered completely out of it.

With anguish and confusion
Pillows became tossed angrily;
Brining about an end to it.

There is need for discussion,
Before completely dismantling;
The bed we've made from it.

Time to speak the unspoken,
Locate what wasn't said;
And put nouns and verbs to it.

It's now or never to show a token
Before we each make single beds;
From the bed we made from it.

# SHEILA

Created by an unprofessional hand
You sit uncomfortably between two chips,
One of which is unknown by name
Whist the other chooses to be anonymous.

You're right there in-between them
With your Indian blue lines blown,
Drifting towards the hairline
You've become separated from the form.

All have left a heavy weight
For the caretaker to carry,
But you must have been the special one
As you sit between her shoulders.

# THIS WAS AND IS LOVE

This, whatever it is,
Sorry, whatever it was:
Passion, Loneliness, Insanity,
Friendship, Subterfuge, Fantasy, Realism;
This brief flirtation with desire and danger,
Has left the characters in unbearable tension.

This, whatever it might have been,
Sorry, what it still is:
Being Smitten, Hooked, Besotted,
And Enamored, Infatuated and Obsessed;
This ongoing need to not be confused,
Has left cynicism to lurk behind their masks.

That,
Sorry, this whatever it was,
Sorry, what this is;
Is having to deal with:
Uncertainty, Chaos, Mystification, Confusion,
And the L Word.

This is unequivocally:
Indisputably, Undeniably, Clearly,
And absolutely unmistakably,
Full of Bewilderment and Disorder,
This is not whatever,
This was and is Love.

# THE ELEPHANT AND THE DOCTOR

A sad three legged elephant
made an appointment to see a Doctor,
the man understood his needs
because his name was Dr Foster.

The elephant explained he wanted
to jump into a puddle,
but having just three legs
it only caused a muddle.

Since the doctor had been to Gloucester
in a shower of rain,
he understood just perfectly
how wellingtons one should gain.

"Great!" exclaimed the elephant
with a smile upon his face
"you get that there is more to do
than win a three legged race."

Dr Foster went to his workshop
a tin shed out the back,
where he made a wooden leg
and fitted it with a strap.

The Elephant was delighted
because races now he could win,
he skipped outside the surgery
and leapfrogged over a bin.

The Doctor got a present
for his new friend he had found,
super large size wellingtons
to protect from water on the ground.

The Doctor and the Elephant
skipped off hand in hand,
on puddle jumping journeys
far across the land.

# ANYWAY

Saw that bird today you know her
What's her face?
Used to live on the East Side
What's her name again?
Anyway
She's not with
What's his name from over the bridge?
Lived by that pub
You know the one
Had a comedy band.
Anyway
They split up
He was having it away
With that woman drove a taxi
The one with glasses
Long blonde hair
Big teeth and eyebrows
Can't remember where she's from.
Anyway
Now she's with the bald guy
From the garage on the roundabout
The one that sells flowers
But closes on a Sunday
It's by that DIY shop
Bought my garden furniture there.
Anyway
You catch my drift yeah
You know who I mean
She works in the hairdressers now
The one up the hill
By the school for naughty boys
Anyway
They split up.

# AND ANYWAY

Saw that Father yesterday
The one with all the Father brothers
Lived on the big dipper
What's that street called again?
The one behind the club
Ran trips to Pontins
Had cabaret and bingo nights.
And anyway
Met that woman
The one with lots of dogs
And a black one with no lead
You know the one?
Has coffee with her friend
Walks about with her mother.
And anyway
She told me
Those doors are locked
They're a fire exit now
You know the ones
By the motorbikes
Next to the café
Now you got to walk around.
And anyway
Bought that bread
With bits on top
Like green straw
Got nuts in
They look like unmentionables
No good for false teeth.
And anyway
Here you are do you want it?

# ONE DEVIL TOWN

The Devil came to Swansea
Jumped into the reel
He wanted to know for himself
How the Jacks did feel.

He met a man on a cliff
That viewed over the Gower
The man said don't rain on me devil
And tell me it's a golden shower.

So he went to get the Cork Ferry
Walked out along the Pier
Only to find it don't run no more
So instead he went for a beer.

The Devil sat with all the drinking folk
In the Queens on the corner
He liked this place in Cymru
Hell itself was not much warmer.

Then he walked on up into the town
Wandered into the busy market
Tried to make cash in hand deals
For souls when they kicked the bucket.

Barabrith and Cockles filled the air
As from the roof came down his brother
Neither of them showed any respect
Hurling books by Iris Gower.

The Swansea Devil was no looser
Won the battle with hands down
As the defeated brother slithered away
He heard the words don't come back you clown.

# CENSUS FOR THE DEVIL

The Devil's daughter came to Swansea
To research and report back,
On why during the last census
Souls from Abertawe Hell did lack.

The first thing that she noticed
Was everywhere named twice,
Two names on the sign posts
Surely that could be a vice.

She sat outside St. Mary's church
Inconspicuously on a bench,
Dressed in Primark's finest
Like any other town wench.

A local man sat next to her
Offering lager from a carrier bag,
While she drank her Tesco's cheapest
He rolled her a three skin fag.

She wasn't there for recruitment
But surely just one damned soul,
And then he showed her kindness
When he offered to share his dole.

He took her over the Eastside
Introduced her to his brothers,
It was obvious to all around
The two were starry eyed lovers.

She compiled her latest findings
Sealed and sent the census back,
With an NB saying sorry Daddy Devil
Staying here I've fallen for a Swansea Jack.

# LONELY DEVIL

A lonely Devil came to Swansea
One Saturday night to see,
If deals were good as rumour said
Buy a soul get one free.

He didn't worry about his cousin
Who used to curse the church,
Now he's locked inside a market
Stuck high up on a perch.

He started looking on The Promenade
Sat atop of the Meridian Tower,
Watching lovers freely locking lips
And one who charged by the hour.

It seemed that everywhere he looked
Couples were in deep embrace,
And so the thought occurred to him
Maybe he'd find a misses in this place.

He went up to the Kingsway
Watched a girl vomit huey into a bin,
That's the one he wickedly thought
Underneath fake Gucci she's head to toe in sin.

He held her hair back from her face
In comfort said there there,
He was liking the new experience
Of pretending to show a woman care.

In a flash she turned crazy on him
Tore his creepy flesh with her nails,
As she landed a Mount-Pleasant slap on his face
She cried that's from all the women of Wales.

# ELLIPSIS IN SHAPE AND FORM

In periods of complete…
  Clarity
  Obviousness
  Lucidity
  Explicitness
At times of absolute…
  Disassociation
  Vagueness
  Abstraction
  Inattention
On occasions of total…
  Comprehension
  Discernment
  Awareness
  Knowledge
During moments of intense…
  Disconnection
  Hibernation
  Severance
  Uncoupling
Through times of the…
  Necessary
  Crucial
  Essential
  Basic
Within points of misunderstanding…
  Conflict
  Misinterpretation
  Variance
  Discord
Beyond days of withdrawal…
  Retreat
  Disengagement
  Cancellation
  Departure

Inside of the ellipsis…
    Cycle
    Rotation
    Sequence
    Phases
In conditions of complete and absolute misunderstanding
During times of clarity and understanding
The original shape and form still exists somewhere...

# ERELONG ELEGIST

The more I deal in pen and rhyme,
more innominatus becomes the pastime.
Furthermore metrical composition,
only authenticates situation.
Oft meanings barely tangible,
intermingled with the unmanageable.
Occasionally the allegoric,
misinterpreted for elegiac.
On occasion a gentle whisper,
other times a water filled blister.
What is it about this poetry malarkey?
that helps relieve momentary ennui.

# FINAL LINE

Outside the boundaries
of
subjectively normal parameters,
there is no blame for death
that metronome still ticks.

        Inside is an entry wound
                with no exit.

No solution to grief
      it is just
a bleeding stigmata
on an absent friend.

Walking away from noise

        has its appeal

here amongst the going and the gone.

You and I are a part of the design
to not be alone in any void


that is the final line........

# I WAS WRONG…

**I**, does not mean, it's all about me.
**I** have had more than my share of:
Mistaken pride in achievement
Bitter pain in loss
Misguided happiness through gain.
**I** have taken what **I** have been given:
Something's received with thanks
Surprising elements that have shocked
Situations **I** did not want.
**I** have foolishly:
Acted for better just to make things worse
Spoken to much and not at all
Let go and held on in the wrong place.
**I** have taken whatever has been thrown:
Compliments with salt for wounds
Rough and uncouth justice
Mud filled with stones.
**I** have had more:
Ill health than well being
Sorrow than joy
Crying than laughter.
**I** have asked for:
Forgiveness for my stupidity
All the malice **I** have received
Bygones to be bygones.
**I** have been told in raging anger:
You always put yourself first
Ignored wrong doings
Blame lies squarely with me.
**I** mourn every minute of every day for:
Loss of flesh and blood
Deprivation to and from my kin
For those **I** carried within.
**I** am left with:
A fathomless abyss of stagnation
Isolation and empty space

Coming last again.
To begin each verse with **I** evidences:
Selfishness
Self-pity
You are right **I** am all about me.
**I** am trying to get you understand:
How deep my sorrow goes
Actions **I** do not know to take
**I** don't know what words **I** should say.
**I** thought **I** could change:
Genetic inheritance
Improve the family line
Give opportunity to make a better life.

# LOCKED SONG

She's in a locked room,
everybody knows her
the one who is the real me
except for me.
There's a list of songs in my head,
tunes with no titles
music and no lyrics
some note and word perfect.
Do you know my song?
The one that starts with me not remembering.
To the me I was before
they all mean something
meant something,
the other me – She knows – but She won't tell.
I try to paint pictures,
inner spectrum hues turn into
muddy memories on a brown palette.
She is prone to freeing herself,
nipping out quickly
stealing my conclusions,
then locks herself and them back in.
She resides inside that room
always looking back at me through dirty windows,
I am stuck on the outside.
When She feels generous,
She might give a memory back.
it's like She is punishing me,
She never gives enough dots
for joining up a whole picture.
Those who work with brains,
they say,
got to focus on who I am now,
not be too concerned about who I was.
This is harder than I can think,
not sure if She feels the same.
She won't tell me.

# ME VS MASS COMMUNICATION

The phone rings, sometimes the voice is;
barely audible with Eastern or Asian accents,
totally unable to pronounce my name.
Sometimes the voice is crisp and clear;
with a British accent,
more than capable of pronouncing my name.
Now and then the anonymous voice is in between the two.

Do I know I need?
PPI
Health
Teeth
Buildings
Contents
Car
Travel
Pet and Mobile Phone Insurance.

Do I know I can get cheaper?
Home Phone
Broadband
Gas
Electricity.

Do I know I can help with?
Poverty in the UK and Europe
World depravation
Feeding starving children
Building a Well
Homelessness
Abuse in all its forms
Homing unwanted pets
Conservation
Regeneration
Raising awareness of numerous diseases.

From some of the above,
Postman delivers do I know/can I help leaflets.

Email spam folder full of get;
Penis enlargement
Less wrinkles
Weight loss
Remedy for baldness
Foreign women seeking British lovers.

Do I know I am?
    A balding wealthy overweight man,
With a small penis looking for a foreign wife?
No I didn't,
No thank-you for the information.

Do I know I have money to give away?
No I didn't,
No I don't.

Do I know I can stop nuisance calls?
Yes I do
Does it work?
No it does not.

Do I know I can block spammers?
Yes I do
Does it work?
No it doesn't they reinvent themselves,
Just as they have reinvented me.

# TOODLE-OO

In my nest there's a Cuckoo
Causing a hullabaloo
I'm fed up with it's pooh
Gonna say so-long-toodle-oo
To that tu-wit-tu-woo.

Gonna learn verbal kung-fu
With the toe of my shoe
I'll kick it up the wazoo
It's gonna meet its waterloo
With no paddle for the canoe.

Gonna wash out with shampoo
Get a new hairdo
Elbow out that cuckoo
With a quick buckaroo
Sneeze it out a-a-at-choo.

# UNTITLED BRAIN POEM

This is a confession
My brain it doesn't work
Sometimes I'm bright as button
Other times I'm a berk.

In the past I filled my brain
Full of facts and diversity
Some I learned along the way
Others in a university.

Nothing prepared me
For my brains explosion
Guess I filled it till it burst
That's my only conclusion.

I've seen very many doctors
Who don't know what to do
Just for once one should say
Sorry I haven't got a clue.

So today I told the truth
Was as honest as can be
Let the symptoms all come out
From deep inside of me.

The doctor that I saw today
He sat and scratched his head
I failed to meet criteria
Based on what I said.

So now I'm on a waiting list
That's over two years long
And I bet in two years' time
They still won't know what's wrong.

I hideaway my troubles
Make it hard to tell
That underneath my cleverness
I really am not well.

# RECORDS WILL DOCUMENT
# A PARODY VILLANELLE

With the expiration of appliance warranty,
As a secondary symptom to the ailment;
The rattling machine has become a parody.

A many sided coin of mystery,
Neither use nor decorative ornament;
With the expiration of appliance warranty.

In a world of theoretically,
Circuits have become deficient;
The rattling machine has become a parody.

Of what the function was previously,
And what it now is the moment here present;
With the expiration of appliance warranty.

The tragedy of this plays comedy,
Has become impossible to circumvent;
The rattling machine has become a parody.

With much confusion and inconsistency,
Records will document.
With the expiration of appliance warranty,
The rattling machine has become a parody.

# FIVE O'CLOCK

Waiting is a game for the patient, of
An unspecified amount of time;
In one way or another,
Time marked always passes.

To another day of waiting,
Impatiently for a response;
Let's look at this seriously,
Leave all politeness to one side.

For pities sake, why silence that,
Instigates irrational behaviour in;
Voicemails left before dawn,
Explaining irrationally waited.

Outside and inside the working day, for
Communications of any kind;
Lost amongst repetitive non-responses,
Over and over again, repeating,
Can someone please communicate?
Knowing silence will come as the reply.

After the clock hits five,
Gone goes any chance;
And another night will bring another day,
In which there will inevitably be,
Non-communication.

# REMIX ON LOOP

Events come and go,
Stories stop making sense.
Who are you? Becomes what are you?
And the audio remix tape
Plays repeatedly on loop.

In experiencing the story alone,
One becomes the incubator
Of the chicken and the egg;
A barking dog, turned mute.

Whilst the Sat-Nav in the mind orders,
Turn left – Do a U turn –
Turn right – Do a U turn –
In 0.0 miles arrive at destination.

Exist unhappily ever after,
In a siege tower contained in a wormhole;
With infinite impossibilities,
In remaining static in an improbable realm.

Where decimated past lives,
Patiently await reincarnation;
And the video remix tape
Plays repeatedly on loop.

# THE STRUGGLE BETWEEN TWO SELVES

There are two selves, who struggle,
In a conflict of interest;
She who is best dominates to win,
Neither do.

The She who holds conversation,
Has an amenable demeanor;
With a willing spirit,
Her attempts are sincere.
She imagines herself,
Articulate and lucid in expression;
A conversation partaker,
If only very rarely.

The She who takes cover,
Apprehensive at every noise;
As susceptible to whispered hushes,
As she is to vociferous noise.
Angst ridden with fear,
She imagines herself;
Able to hide away,
If only a safe place existed.

The two selves are pursued,
By a cat as black as carbon;
With quilting needle claws,
That tap as it stalks.
Often disguised as a shadow,
The absence of light;
Assists the game of stalking,
Allowing it to swoop suddenly,
Attacking when least expected.

The she who holds conversation,
And she who takes cover;
Are equally as vulnerable,
To damage and molestation,
From the black as carbon feline.

# DEPRESSION DELEGATION IN A TWO DIMENSIONAL VILLANELLE BOX

In a two dimensional depression,
One tends to become nefarious;
And is lost within responsibility delegation.

Attitudes are somewhat of accusation,
But conceptual attitudes are the consensus;
In a two dimensional depression.

To add to much indignation,
The gynecological monster is zealous;
And is lost within responsibility delegation.

Bogged down in referral and administration,
The thought of it all is tremulous;
In a two dimensional depression.

There is so much time for contemplation,
And little time for discourse;
When lost within responsibility delegation.

With one small indiscretion,
The man of one's dreams becomes Morpheus;
In a two dimensional depression.

No one to hear confession,
When one is unceremonious.
In a two dimensional depression,
One becomes lost within responsibility delegation.

# A SLICE OF VILLANELLE CAKE

Into the poem called a slice of cake,
Each black letter adds to the debate;
Check if the heroine is still half awake.

With cream on top, not dairy but fake,
Oozing over the sides of her plate;
Into the poem called a slice of cake.

Get her up, her bed she has to make,
Nudge her quick, before it's too late;
Check if the heroine is still half awake.

Pinch her eyes open, a lot is at stake,
No matter she is weary going sedate;
Into the poem called a slice of cake.

Give her loud bells, all she can take,
There is no more time left to wait;
Check if the heroine is still half awake.

She is aware great things are at stake,
She knows all about pouring love hate;
Into the poem called a slice of cake.

She is not to sleep through this earthquake,
She has to get up and go before it's too late.
Into the poem called a slice of cake,
Check if the heroine is still awake.

# PUCKER UP AND...

Talk to me now
And we need never be silent again,
Wink your eye at me once
And we won't ever have to cry again.
Purse your lips
And we can sip red wine,
Enevelop my hand
And we can be brave.
Step out of the shadows
And we can move into the light,
Walk by my side
And we can be equals.
Talk, Wink, Purse,
Envelop, Step, Walk,
Pucker up
And
Move up
Into the light.

# MIDSUMMER DESPONDENCE AND NO SHOES

I've become despondent
In the village way of life,
Grown to be nauseous
Of existing without verve;
Why do I smile unrealistically?
At the village world and his wife,
And not scream at her husband
Who gropes me with no nerve.

I think I am becoming
One of whom I've come to hate,
This became clear to me
At the last on the green fete;
I paid over a fiver for a cappuccino
With no chocolate sprinkles on top,
And bought things that are cheaper
Brand new from the shop.

Now I know I am a widow
Fast approaching full maturity,
And at this time of my life
I should be seeking security;
But then today in a local shop
Whilst standing in the posh que,
It suddenly overcame me
And I knew what I had to do.

I went back to my pretty little house
With its lawn all clipped and neat;
Took off my painful leather shoes
That have only ever hurt my feet;
And made a promise to myself
To stop pretending to be what I'm not,
Galvanized my positive intentions
And prepared to move me from this spot.

With shoeless steps I wandered
Over my neat green lawn,
And brought back the girl in me
I thought had long since gone;
Imagining and remembering how it feels
To live in a busy bustling city,
That was all I needed to make sure
I'll be leaving here with no pity.

# CIGARETTES WERE SMOKED

With longing and suspense,
The experienced woman
Spoke in playful pleasantries,
She could sense her own breath
Filling the air with things unsaid,
Things one can't say
Not until one is sure;
That signals are not misread
That sexuality radar is correct,
So forced was her control
Her very libido ached.
The passing of a cigarette lighter
Moved the situation onto another level,
As she brushed her experienced finger
Lightly over the inexperienced hand of her desire,
Accidently on purpose sending electric
I want to take you now sensations,
Tingling from the finger of experience
Into the hand of the inexperienced,
And back again through
Two bodies tense from desires.
She longed to be past
The furtive eye contact,
And come and get me if you dare smiles,
Past the first kiss
And the exploration through cloth;
To be beyond the awkwardness of
Undoing zips and buttons
And the pulling of T-shirts over heads,
To the bit where she wished,
If only she had worn sexier underwear.
Finding it harder and harder
To not just dive in,
This game had gone on for so long
Both women had danced around,
Testing the water without the bravery

To just get on with it;
Until not so much out of the blue
Or even all of a sudden,
But certainly with urgency
Engaged with deep lustful need,
Open lips met with
Mouths and tongues probing.
With fervor and delight
Shiny pearls were rubbed,
Rolled and softly drawn upon
Sucked like a sherbet pip,
With each movement of their tongues
Sexual senses writhed and raised,
Until sensation reached a quivering peak
And they folded against each other,
Cigarettes were smoked
And words of experience spoken.

# WHY?

Arriving at a river and
Discovering no bridges,
Not a single stepping stone
Or shallow ford to walk.
A further enquiry followed by
Just one more question
Answered with another question,
Replying with a question
As requests turn to demands
Following query after query.
The empty space between inquiries
Filled with insecurities and possibly,
Enveloped in the bondages
Of false hope and optimism.
Becoming ever-more the fugitive
Refraining from speaking any further,
For fear of something unequivocal
Tainted with tears and antagonism.
The mouth falls shut
Wishing to speak no further,
Of mechanisms that caused sorrow
During the labor of love,
There is only backing into a corner.
All that remains is to halt reactions
Concede happiness is incomprehensible,
Curtail, make less painful the cut,
Accept the bridge was imaginary
Conceded to defeat and move on.
Ending with an unanswerable question
Answered with an unanswerable question,
Why?

# ENCEPHALOMALACIA

The Id, Her, Myself and I,
On becoming yet another medicus term;
She is lost inside the vox populi.

Presenting with confusion of eye,
Bruised around socket and filled with alarm;
The Id, Her, Myself and I.

Being seized, with what it might imply,
With loss of composure and calm;
She is lost inside the vox populi.

With knowing the answers, but not why,
Only further brings more questions to disarm;
The Id, Her, Myself and I.

To live with this thing, I now must try,
Gone is all about me that once was calm;
She is lost inside the vox populi.

And now, as I attempt to understand why,
Came the aching of body and loss of all charm;
The Id, Her, Myself and I,
She is lost inside the vox populi.

# ONE DAY SOON

When the high northern wind blows,
And leaves shy away from first snows;
Could I join you in the place nobody knows?
Where tomorrow's river still freely flows.
So we may sit, cuddled upon its icy banks,
Enveloped in love, and for that give thanks;
And you can give me one of your special winks,
That tells me what your warm heart thinks.
Whilst in our ears, a songbird sings,
Protecting our love with spread bronzed wings;
Then we'll move along to much better things,
Knowing exactly for us, what tomorrow brings.

# FOR YOU MY UNTRUE DUCK

You instigated an irresistible itch
Requiring a deep down scratch;
I willingly became your secret lover
And you clawed at me like no other.

Served me up as a best cold dish
Striking deep into my hearts flesh;
You burrowed harsh and dug deep
Brining to life nightmares from my sleep.

With your twisted form of deception
You clouded and veiled my intuition;
Put your deceivers knife in with a twist
Whilst lovingly kissing my wrist.

Such a fool was I to trust
Your love and your lust;
For when out our secret came
On me you fully placed the blame.

Out of it all I've had to gain
Is heartache, threats, tears and pain;
Released yet still in the prison
Of will I never learn my lesson?

That when along comes someone like you
Saying it's worth it I love you;
That I should take a view from outside
Before allowing of burrowing inside.

Next time I must not be so eager
Until all becomes much clearer;
Hold off and not allow myself to feel
Until I'm sure that love is real.

That if it doesn't walk like a duck
Or look like a duck, it probably isn't a duck;
That if it looks too good to be true
It's probably just like another you.

# EMOTIONAL VAMPIRE

To a poisonous lead point,
Sharpened claws dipped in Indian Ink,
Poked their mark;
Leaving blue dots of dangerous love,
Invisible to the naked eye,
Only evident to the marked,
And the keeper of souls.

Blood of nourishment,
Fed upon with fervor and desire,
Caused a coveted trail of plasma;
To trickle across collar bones,
Pooling under aching breasts,
Drying congealed and viscid,
Burning the soul like acid.

The reanimated emotional vampire,
Plump from the feast of love,
Withdrew into the small hours;
Whilst it's depleted quarry,
From the wounds of claw and bite,
Lay sapped and bleeding,
At the result of desire.

# VULVARLY UNFAMILIAR SIGHT

Still the bitten fingers bleed,
Emotion held captive in chains and shackles,
And the hand retracts in deed.

Destined to not ever succeed,
Metaphorical legs ironed and glued in madness,
Still the bitten fingers bleed.

A branch offered from the olive tree,
With aching heart, high toes and outstretched fingers,
And the hand retracts in deed.

Now grow tall the nurtured seed,
Removed itself to far away but forever lingers,
Still the bitten fingers bleed.

Crossed fingers in expectancy and need,
Begging dialogue with assaulting diatribe mingles,
And the hand retracts in deed.

No matter the strength of plead,
Outreaching for the company of forgiveness,
Still the bitten fingers bleed,
And the hand retracts in deed.

# ALONGSIDE COATS

A vinyl copy of Tubular Bells
Plays and st…i…ck…s…
Jumping too - - -
And introducing,
The coats taken and left behind
In a party that has wound down.

Amongst the secrets,
Whoever they are, they bleed,
With wounds that hurt
In the silence of the night
Like coats forgotten,
They once belonged.

Balls and chains
Drag along the path,
Leaving an evidence trail
To a closed door.
Faces in the windows
Stare out with rejected eyes.

In the eternal stench of silence,
No! . . . . . .
In silent rejection
Repeatedly breaks the air.
Behind shutters
Eye water falls.

The word
That is not enough
Is all that is left,
Hanging in the memory
Alongside coats
Left behind.

# FACEBOOK

Self-proclaimed virtual reality of carefully orchestrated creative consciousness's.
Measures worth through sheer volume activity, cookie trails feeding information.
False organic machine monitors all visits, activity log monitored with vagueness.
Groups
Discuss
Others
Status
Users
Pseudo humans appearing sincere advertise products based on mistaken searches.
Looking briefly at interesting photograph starts bombardments of must have buys.
Users may join common interest groups feeding more information regarding likes.
Sponsored by
Face - ache
Like button
Create page
Life event
Like page
Page feed
Interests
Network
Activity
Sharing
Groups
Remove
Friends
Delete
Add
Real life
Face to face
Meetings for real
Welcome to the real world
Speak with words not ephemeral text.

.

.

.

Oh
Seedy
Diamond
Leading with domination
Controlling with preoccupation
Interfering of thinking theories driving
Irresistible urges come overwhelming impulses drive
Purely empowerment produces chaotic disturbances of malady
Resting cluttered commotion muddling inside fracas
Problem splinter refraction in brightness
Producing sensational luminosity
Colorless and precious
Minerals
Shiny
By
Oh
Seedy
Diamond
Obviously with influence
Hold back keeping power in check
Manipulative imagination sending imaginary
Authentication on impulse using unfeigned directions
Unaffected by reality compulsion overpowers reveling in idealism
Frequently performance fueled uncertainty of actions
Avoidance can confuse roles successfully again
Resulting in vaguely relative critique
Imbalanced in remainder
Diamond
Seedy
Oh

.

.

.

# BLOOD FLOWED

Eruption came suddenly,
Blood flowed,
Death came
Then left,
Taking tears and memory
Leaving existence in place
Laughter and crying
Completely gone
But not forgotten,
Resentment for the fighter
Every minute of everyday
Reminders of former self
Repeated in words
Highlighter by pictures
A self portrait
Of an explosion
In the head.

# WINTER

With my beautiful silver transparent wings,
At first I glide gently and slowly in.
Brining with me the shortness of day,
Extending the darkness of night.
Moving air quickly with my natural force,
Trees sway to resist me.
A fight lost to the prevailing of my wind.

Branches whisper to nature's growth,
It's about to happen soon.
Although exactly when is unknown,
But the series of events has begun.
The cause of important changes,
Nestled in between autumn and spring.
I am winter feel the chill in speaking my name.

Sometimes mild most often severe,
Harsh, wet and cold.
Birds have left to avoid my language,
I can and will, kill and destroy.
The very old and the brand new are first to respond,
As I bring with me, hypothermia, novo virus, hunger,
Seasonal depression, rain and black ice.

The back story is more purposeful,
Holding the real need for my existence.
I have poetic justice at my disposal,
The ironic twist of fate dealt by nature's players.
I am the allegory that is winter,
Lengthening with every passing year.
My beauty destroys, aids and envelopes all.

Through my harsh famine months,
Communities huddle in uncertainty of their survival.
Starvation not an uncommon event.
I will cover you,
With my beautiful silver transparent wings.
Until astronomical events are evidenced,
In the mating of animals and tiny green shoots.

Through the time when the sun on the horizon,
Appears at its low altitude.
Calendar based methods cannot pin me down,
Nature herself has lost control over me.
The appearance of green buds and crocus,
No longer mark the end of my arrest.
In deception calm and warmth are felt.

# TO CALL FROM BEHIND THE WALL

To lead
To check
To think
To see

My nature is to lead with suspicion,
Any gift horse checked for fleas.
There's always more to what I'm thinking,
More than what you think you see.

Call for deeds, from truth
Equality

Dark times often call for dark deeds,
In light being softly faithful and true.
The black swan glides behind equally as far,
The white swan leads forward bravely.

Without defenses
Weapons
Actions
Things

Do you come with painful weapons
Intent to injure without care?
If so beware
Things are not always what they seem
My strength is a secret weapon of choice.

Often in frustration
Often with pain
…kindness,
Fright.

Painful is bearable at a cost,
Kindness as the breaker.
Everyone has something worth fighting for,
The costs not always first agreed.

Having relief
Having action
Having freedom
Having change

Have you come to injure or relieve?
Actions given time will tell all, reveal.
I feel the change, it is a coming,
Time blows freely through my hair.
Timely waiting
Timely close
Timely right

# TIME OUT

Time spent waiting behind an impenetrable wall,
Gate keys close at hand.
Waiting for signals to be given,
To open and peer out.

To call freely
To communicate often
Have choice
Possess time
Feel free
To hold, eternally
Be equal
Be brave

To not be anxious
...alone
...not without
Timid, scarred
Wanting
To not be contradictory
Be conflicting

To call freely and walk out
To leave behind the wall
To acknowledge the signals
To cast off restrictions
To move with freedom
To be honest and open
To speak openly
To be too...

# SELF-PERFORMED GLOSSECTOMY

The more I try to not disappoint,
Trudge through the mire happily;
The more I disappoint.

In trying to guess what you want,
Feed your needs emotionally;
The more I try to not disappoint.

You disguise being so distant,
In words spoken artificially;
The more I disappoint.

Becoming ever more resistant,
To ice winds blowing northerly;
The more I try to not disappoint.

With a mouth washed in disinfectant,
In words spoken accordingly;
The more I disappoint.

Trying to avoid uninvited harassment,
With self-performed glossectomy.
The more I try to not disappoint,
The more I disappoint.

# SHE SECRETLY SPITS FIRE

In dramatic monologue
continuous and allegorical,
She scorches
with her tongue,
Hot air
of irrational strength,
Burns cochlea
blistering on touch.

Hot coals she spits
igniting much distrust,
Smothering friendships
in lighted fires,
Secretly fanned
from smolder to blaze,
Whilst she hides
within a smokescreen.

When her crooked
hand extends,
Beware the warmth
in her voice,
For encircle you
secretly she will,
In the fire
from her tongue.

# FOR YOU

You hide,
Away all your hurts;
But they are breaking you,
Wearing you down.

You stand,
With a straight spine;
But are curling up inside,
Like a twisting cord.

You sing along,
To songs about finding love;
But your heart,
It no longer believes.

You look,
Everyone square in the eyes;
But your stomach rolls,
Aches with fear.

You say,
You don't want to talk about it;
But your eyes,
They won't shut up.

You stay,
In a place you call home;
But your feet,
Are ready to walk.

You repeat,
I'm good, no worries;
That's just not true,
Unleash yourself, open up.

# AT 4AM

A myriad of stars
Silently live and die,
Interrupted by a single
Red flashing light,
Taking its passengers
To a destination,
The sky watcher
Can only imagine.
Orion's belt
Holds up the trousers
Of darkness,
Until the blouse
Of daylight,
Drops gently over
Its girth.

# BEFORE I DIE PLEASE LET ME CRY!

Imagine a world, in which you cannot cry
A world in which your throat dries,
The oxygen going into your lungs
Is small and insufficient
Body rocks
Nails dig into palms
Desperation fills heart
Thoughts disjointed
Breathing deep
Still breathing deeper.
Knowing it would cleanse,
If only it would happen.

Imagine knowing you need it, trying to force
Tears to come out,
Pain
Shaking
Trembling
Distress
Hurt
Discontent
None will escape out,
Tears are trapped.

Before I die
I do not want,
Reconciliation
Wealth
Health
Happiness
Love
I want to
Cry with uncontrollable emotions.

Whimper
Blubber Howl
Bawl
Snivel
Weep
Shed tears over and over again.

# FLUFFF...

If fluff has the freedom to fly
Why the surprise when it gets in an eye

I've had enough of fluff
No really I hate the stuff

It's worse than rouge pubic hair
It gets and lives everywhere

We once had a purple fluff phase
No it's not funny it lasted for days

Fluff is not on the list of beauty and charms
When on a night of passion it's stuck underarms

It can be the catalyst for asthma
One of life's mysteries and anathema

Fluff can be a noun a verb an adjective
Depending on where it chooses to live

Belly buttons are one of its favorite places
And for no good reason it sticks to faces

Fluff that gets stuck between toes
Comes from socks that everyone knows

But where does fluff come from down the lavatory
Surely fluff isn't a component of pee

Where does fluff come from that falls from the sky
Just by luck of the draw gets stuck in an eye

The most mysterious fluff of all
Is not the fluff on the floor in the hall

Or gathering in quantity under the bed
It's the fluff that comes out from ones head

Is fluff mentioned in the periodic table
I'm sure it would put itself there if it was able

It gets everywhere that damned stuff
I for one have had enough of fluff

# SMALL PRINT

Oh dear lord won't you bring me
a means to many ends.
I've offended my family
and pissed of my friends.

The walls of my life's work
they are closing in.
Like yesteryears food scraps
rotting in a compost bin.

A publisher once said send poems
to go in anthology.
The very small indeed print said
You get no royalty.

I try to be a good girl
try hard not to smoke.
But living to high standards
is a don't get it joke.

I'll visit the opticians
get some glasses to see.
A clearer view of you out there
and a closer look at me.

When my day of judgment comes
if it's not here right now.
Remember I'm a mere human
a daft and silly cow.

Mirror mirror on my wall

What dreams you catch

Promoting a fantasy

Reflected in sand

Transmitter of reflection

The dream to be

Fairest of them all

The illusionist clone

Builds castles in the air

# SAPPHO'S ROMANCE

Keeping you close a pointless endeavor,
As your intentions were to always to return there,
Risks were taken in the showing of feeling;
Endings of happiness always there and impending,
No was the intention beforehand and forever.

In moments of the buckling of knees,
Somewhere was lost the need to please.

Giving and receiving of moments chaste,
Outpoured reactions to attraction with haste,
Now to never know if there was a real chance,
Ended is the brief but wonderful Sappho's romance.

# ALL I WANT...

Is a warm home
With a cat and dog,
And a person who loves me alone
Who likes to cuddle and snog.

I want an attractive handy-person
To keep me warm in bed,
And to make the odd excursion
Into what's inside my head.

Someone who is a faithful lover
With an kind honest heart,
Who wants me and no other
From the very start.

I know that's requesting
The most unlikely and improbable,
But it doesn't stop me looking
For someone whose adorable.

But then I met my handy-person
Who said they really loved me to,
I believed all their expression
Then discovered it was untrue.

So now I'm left wondering
If I set my sights too high,
So many unanswered questions
Oh how they make me sigh.

Got bitten by that which I desire
Forgetting I want never gets,
I've tried putting aside what I desire
Even abandoned wanting pets.

But still I can't shake it away
The hope that I will find,
On another bright sunny day
A handy-person true and kind.

And that's all I want
Is what I never get.

# A LITTLE BIT OF TANKA

Swashbuckling hero
I'm over here come now
rescue me from
this boring monotony
take me to never land.

*

Strong on the face
travelling westerly
the cobwebs
blow nicely into air
cleansing mind soothing soul.

*

Clue in title
mobile easily moved
one bar is left
battery says not
going anywhere for now.

*

Ecru a rule
no purple approved
orange vetoed
the ecclesiastical
in beige rules.

*

The evidence came to pass
a sanctum existence
drifted like footprints
washed away in
granular sand.

*

Across the way
twenty six windows glow
occupants unknown
strangers never meeting
look into each other.

*

Cesi n'est pas
a juxtaposition
or une pipe
relatively speaking
painting with words.

*

In the quiet time
foxes cry like new babies
dustbins fall
under darks shelter
right to roam prevails.

*

# WHIFFLING HAIKU

For flight I am
still hopefully
constructing it.

Wings almost near
production stage
post design.

More mechanism
than fantasy dream
wings design.

No test flight
just faith required
to take off.

# B&H IN LAUNDRY HAIBUN

Whoever used the washing machine before me also washed their cigarettes. I shake my favourite black skirt, a clean double washed filter falls to the ground. The bit of paper hanging of it has a B&H logo on it, it's faded but there. I contemplate bunging it all in the tumble dryer and leaving bits of stringy tobacco for the next person. I can't do it; I was brought up with better morals than that. I give the washing machine a good clean out, shake tobacco off my clothes and load it for a second wash. I stand guard and watch in case someone changes the settings (as can be the case), another resident comes in. I tell her of my tobacco nightmare. My frustration turns to anger when she tells me. The woman who used the machine before me is in church for the Good Friday Service.

> Does heaven welcome
> Messy Christians inside
> Forgiving laundry sin?

# ON THAT NOTE...

Eyes gently close, all else excluded.
Rhythm begins to flow, it's a rinky tinky tinky,
someone's tinkling the ivories, Oh yeah
good ole rag time blues.
This is the day when life will surely change,
gotta have a dream.

Feet start to tap
shoulders begin to move
both up and down
one and then the other
side to side in rhythmic succession.
Body spins around
hips sway
left to right
circle around and around
arms outstretched
body spins around
smells from the bar
mix with dance floor sweat.
Tingling travels
through core
down to toes
up to neck
into head and down again.

CD stops playing,
eyes open,
day falls into night
on that note
nothing's changed.

# BRIDGES ARE ALREADY BURNING

Bridges are already burning,
Out on the frontier;
A key is slowly turning.

No longer comes a ringing
Telling you are near,
Bridges are already burning.

Flames impossible in quelling,
The sound is very clear;
A key is slowly turning.

Tears keep downward rolling
In refusal to clearly hear,
Bridges are already burning.

Deep within the scolding,
Trapped inside with fear;
A key is slowly turning.

As the truth begins unfolding
With words from yesteryear,
Bridges are already burning
A key is slowly turning.

# MOVING ON

Within the lightening point of the departing night,
Behind oblique shadows that differentiate,
Where a voice calls from inside pure light.

Encouraging choice of leave or fight,
Cautioning, make careful and be considerate;
Within the lightening point of the departing night.

Where a new horizon is within sight
And yesterday's stars brightly tessellate,
Where a voice calls from inside pure light.

Come, the time is now and right
To break from the perpetuate,
Within the lightening point of the departing night.

Let the wind lift gently up in flight,
Quandaries of choice it can eradicate,
Where a voice calls from inside pure light.

Choose where footprints are gentle and slight,
And the breath breathed is delicate;
Within the lightening point of the departing night,
Where a voice calls from inside pure light.

# ENTHUSIASTIC DRAMAS

Took my dramas down to the park
Tried to ease them out of the dark;
On a swing I pushed them high,
Until they almost touched the blue sky.

Spun them around on a witches hat
Only for them to vomit, fact after fact;
We had a picnic, I fed them reasoning,
Told them why they should be leaving.

I laughed at them, right in their face,
Expecting them to run off at a pace;
They followed me home, as bold as brass,
Enthused at their role in the farce.

Inanimate my dramas are definitely not,
They are an on the go, active lot;
So very full of enthusiastic life loving,
If only they weren't so emotionally involving.

They keep up with their passionate interests,
I continue to bombard them with eagerness;
Tried being rid of them through indifference,
But enthusiastic dramas feed forgetfulness.

# HOWLING PETALS

Teeth make slits in stems
One after one God's eyes make a chain
Disconnected others lace up their boots
Trample
Destroy
No coherent structure in the rampage
Bombardment continues
Till each petal is composted
An odyssey of disconnection achieved
Too many nights
Starring at the moon
Binding chaos into order
Disjointed
Irrational
Without punctuation
Past influences at the fore
Unified in own importance
A comedy of divine proportions
Mooning around with no particular purpose
Until comes full stop.

# KILLERS AT DAWN

As first light broke on the horizon
Screams filled the air,
Shrills of pain rang out.
The victim scurried along the frosty ground,
Last attempts to flee thwarted.
Encircling and blocking escape routes,
Sharp black swords pierced through flesh,
Light footed attackers came in for the kill.
Over and over with swift movement and precession,
Until the victim lay helpless,
Last breath a quiet shrill.
Perpetrators stood atop the body
Ripping flesh from bone.
Having had their fulfilment,
They sat on a wall overlooking the dead.
With no remorse they proudly preened,
Moved on as if nothing had happened.
Leaving the victim with inners exposed,
Bloodied
Torn
Fed upon
And dead.

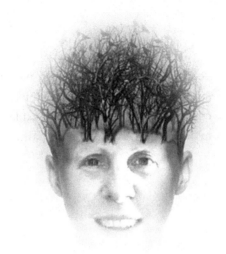

# BIRDS IN THE BELFRY

When birds are singing in my head,
When I can't remember what I've said;
When I get confused and can't understand,
I think of us and our common ground.

I think of you every single day,
What could have happened had we our way;
We both couldn't manage the endless fight,
With should we try and stay overnight.

I never meant to fuck with your head,
I was too afraid to take you into my bed;
Couldn't handle the thought of telling you,
I'm so very ill don't want to burden you.

But know this my could have been lover,
You are inside my head like no other;
I often think long and hard about you,
And all the things we never got to do.

The birds in my belfry sing out your name,
They chirp it out loud with no same;
Please come back just once, so I can explain,
Why for us both I caused such pain.

# JACK TOPOPHILIA

My title is inconsequential;
I'm a dabbler-holic poet.
If name is important to you;
Jack of all types – lover of place
Fits purpose best.

Attics and cellars are full;
Boxes containing consonants and vowels,
Labelled acronyms too zingers
Jabber in the background
Awaiting call to service.

Counter transference;
That old double edged sword.
Misinterpretation;
Make of that what you will,
Dabblers of critique think on.

If poetry is set fire to;
Is that destruction or deconstruction?
If poetry brings anger or happiness;
Is that bad or good?
Does understanding and misunderstanding not serve just the same?

Call me an Illywacker;
A miserable git and ignore.
Call me Intriguing;
Joyful and pleasant.
And happily consider this;
Whatever your interpretation and critique
The dabbler-holic poets
Work here is done.

This may be The End,
Or another beginning;
Life's been one long round,
Of behind things hiding,
Obscuring of the face,
And much recreating.
This may be another ending
Or again the beginning
Of another ending...

Printed in the United States
By Bookmasters